UNDERSTANDING
KAZUO ISHIGURO

Understanding Contemporary British Literature
Matthew J. Bruccoli, Series Editor

UNDERSTANDING
Kazuo
ISHIGURO

Brian W. Shaffer

UNIVERSITY OF SOUTH CAROLINA PRESS

© 1998 University of South Carolina

Cloth edition published by the University of South Carolina Press, 1998
Paperback edition published in Columbia, South Carolina,
by the University of South Carolina Press, 2008

www.sc.edu/uscpress

Manufactured in the United States of America

17 16 15 14 13 12 11 10 09 08   10 9 8 7 6 5 4 3 2 1

The Library of Congress has cataloged the cloth editions as follows:

Shaffer, Brian W., 1960–
    Understanding Kazuo Ishiguro / Brian W. Shaffer.
      p. cm. — (Understanding contemporary British literature)
    ISBN 1-57003-215-7
    1. Ishiguro, Kazuo, 1954– —Criticism and interpretation. I. Title.
  II. Series.
    PR6059.S5Z87   1998
    823'.914—dc21   97-33891

ISBN 978-1-57003-794-8 (pbk)

To Rachel, Hannah, and Ruth

CONTENTS

EDITOR'S PREFACE

The volumes of *Understanding Contemporary British Literature* have been planned as guides or companions for students as well as good nonacademic readers. The editor and publisher perceive a need for these volumes because much of the influential contemporary literature makes special demands. Uninitiated readers encounter difficulty in approaching works that depart from the traditional forms and techniques of prose and poetry. Literature relies on conventions, but the conventions keep evolving; new writers form their own conventions—which in time may become familiar. Put simply, *UCBL* provides instruction in how to read certain contemporary writers—identifying and explicating their material, themes, use of language, point of view, structures, symbolism, and responses to experience.

The word *understanding* in the titles was deliberately chosen. Many willing readers lack an adequate understanding of how contemporary literature works; that is, what the author is attempting to express and the means by which it is conveyed. Although the criticism and analysis in the series have been aimed at a level of general accessibility, these introductory volumes are meant to be applied in conjunction with the works they cover. They do not provide a substitute for the works and authors they introduce, but rather prepare the reader for more profitable literary experiences.

M. J. B.

ACKNOWLEDGMENTS

I wish to acknowledge a special debt of gratitude to Jennifer Brady and Jo Ellyn Clarey, who read and provided invaluable feedback on the entire manuscript. I would like also to thank the following colleagues and friends for providing helpful feedback on one or more chapters of this study: Robert Entzminger, Robert Franciosi, Bruce Krajewski, Michael Leslie, Cynthia Marshall, Tod Marshall, and Sandra McEntire. Thanks are also due Rhodes College for providing me with two Summer Faculty Development Endowment Grants, which aided in the timely completion of this project and with funds to defray the cost of indexing. My mother and late father also deserve recognition for encouraging me to pursue this study. Kieron Swaine and Lisa Jennings challenged me to think about contemporary British literature and culture in a new way. And Kazuo Ishiguro was kind enough to answer countless questions—by letter, phone, fax, and in person—about his fictions and about himself. Finally, I wish to thank my wife, Rachel, for generously sharing with me her insights on Ishiguro's work, and my two daughters, Hannah and Ruth, for their patience and for being boundless sources of joy and inspiration.

UNDERSTANDING
KAZUO ISHIGURO

CHAPTER ONE

Understanding
Kazuo Ishiguro

Few writers dare to say so little of what they mean
as Ishiguro.

Mark Kamine,
"A Servant of Self-Deceit," 22

In a century of British prose fiction heralded and shaped by
such transplanted authors as the Polish Joseph Conrad and the
American Henry James, it nevertheless may come as a surprise
that Kazuo Ishiguro, a Japanese-born writer, now ranks among
England's most distinguished contemporary novelists. Born in
Nagasaki in 1954, Ishiguro received one of England's most pres-
tigious literary awards, the Booker Prize, in 1989.[1] The son of a
Japanese oceanographer whose work attracted the attention and
interest of the British government, Kazuo Ishiguro left Japan at
six years old with his family and settled in Guildford, Surrey.
What was to be a one-year visit evolved into a permanent move;
Ishiguro became an English resident and has remained one. Reflecting upon his upbringing from the perspective of adulthood,
Ishiguro views himself as having received a "typical English
education"[2] and a "typical middle-class Southern English upbringing."[3] In the early years of school, however, he experienced
what might be called culture shock, finding himself "a curiosity
in the playground" and adjusting to a new reality in which he
was not to see "another non-English person" for years.[4] His "dis-

tinct background" of being brought up English "by Japanese parents in a Japanese-speaking home" probably accounts for the author's sense of not thinking "entirely like" an English-born writer, of having perspectives that are "slightly different."[5] This bicultural upbringing also probably accounts for Ishiguro's feeling of being a "homeless writer," of lacking a natural constituency or audience, of being neither "very English" nor "very Japanese": "I had no clear role, no society or country to speak for or write about. Nobody's history seemed to be my history." For this reason Ishiguro is most comfortable identifying himself as an international writer.[6]

Ishiguro studied English and philosophy at Kent University, graduating with Honors in 1978, and creative writing with novelist-critic Malcolm Bradbury at the University of East Anglia, graduating in 1980. In his twenties he worked as a social worker with the homeless in Glasgow and London hostels. In 1986 he married Lorna Anne MacDougall. They live in the greater London area with their daughter, Naomi, who was born in 1992.

Ishiguro began his artistic career writing short stories and television dramas. However, it is his four intricately crafted, hauntingly evocative, psychologically compelling novels for which he is best known and most critically esteemed. His first novel, *A Pale View of Hills* (1982), concerns the post–World War Two remembrances of a middle-aged Japanese woman, Etsuko, who has made a permanent move to an English "country house." It focuses in particular on Etsuko's relationship with her two daughters (from two marriages), one of whom has recently visited from London and the other of whom has recently committed suicide. In the background lurks the nuclear devastation of Nagasaki and Etsuko's painful personal history. The novel was enthusiastically received and won the 1983 Winifred Holtby Award of the Royal Society of Literature. Ishiguro's second novel, *An Artist of the Floating World* (1986), centers on an aging Japanese painter, Masuji Ono, who reminisces and agonizes over his career as an artist in Japan during the war years. Like Etsuko, he also has two daughters as well as unacknowledged regrets and unarticulated feelings of guilt about his earlier wartime activities. He too must alter his personal history in order to make it more palatable—for himself as well as for his readers. The novel was short-listed for the Booker Prize and was awarded the Whitbread Book of the Year Award.

Ishiguro attributes his early success to good timing and to getting "a very easy ride from the critics":

> The big milestone was the Booker Prize going to Salman Rushdie in 1981 for *Midnight's Children.* He had previously been a completely unknown writer. That was a really symbolic moment and then everyone was suddenly looking for other Rushdies. It so happened that around this time I brought out *A Pale View of Hills.* Usually first novels disappear . . . without a trace. Yet I received a lot of attention, got lots of coverage, and did a lot of interviews. . . . because I had this Japanese face and this Japanese name. . . .[7]

As if reacting to this profitable ("publicity-wise" and "career-wise") yet encumbering and confining identification as an

Anglo-Japanese novelist ("Like any writer, I resist being put in a group"),[8] Ishiguro followed his two "Japanese" novels with a third novel that he describes as "more English than English."[9] *The Remains of the Day* (1989) focuses on English characters residing on English soil. Ishiguro's best-known work to date, this novel of manners concerns Mr. Stevens, the head butler of an English estate, Darlington Hall, who motors across England to meet with a female ex-coworker, Miss Kenton. This drive, taken in 1956, affords Stevens the opportunity to remember and understand better his earlier professional experience "in service" during the 1930s and 1940s. Ishiguro focuses on the butler rather than on the more influential master of such an estate because "The butler is a good metaphor for the relationship of very ordinary, small people to power."[10] This third novel represents a refinement and perfection of the narrative techniques and psychological portraits of its two predecessors. Indeed, Stanley Kauffmann does not overstate the case when he asserts, "About *The Remains of the Day* it is possible to risk the word 'perfect.' Ishiguro's book belongs with the best of English fiction that treats the English class system with combined satire and relish, with perception of both its cruelty and its rigorous ethos, as a distillation of English history."[11] The novel was awarded the Booker Prize in 1989 and was produced as a film by Merchant-Ivory Productions in 1993. Ruth Prawer Jhabvala adapted the novel for the screen; and Anthony Hopkins and Emma Thompson starred as Stevens and Kenton. The film, which was nominated for eight Academy Awards, further enhanced Ishiguro's growing reputation.

His fourth novel, *The Unconsoled* (1995), winner of the

Cheltenham Prize, marks a significant shift in direction for the author. This work centers on a world-famous English pianist, Ryder, who visits an unidentified central European city for a few days in order to give a recital and to help the city resolve its nagging artistic and identity crises. This shift in Ishiguro's focus is not merely one of terrain—from Japan and England to continental Europe—but one of tone and temperament as well: in *The Unconsoled* the elegant Jamesian prose of the earlier novels is replaced with a disturbing Kafkaesque dreamscape, just as the short and traditional novel form is abandoned for an epic and experimental form. Yet even in this novel issues of memory, desire, and self-deception are of central concern. Indeed, Galen Strawson's remark about *Remains*—that it is a "finely nuanced and at times humorous study of repression"[12]—applies equally well to *The Unconsoled.*

Thus far, Ishiguro's work has been translated into twenty-seven foreign languages, and the author has received significant international recognition: Italy's Premio Scanno for Literature (1995); the Order of the British Empire (O.B.E.) for services to literature (1995); and honorary doctorates from the Universities of Kent (1990) and East Anglia (1995). At present the author restricts himself to writing full-length novels and filmscripts; he is at work on a new novel and on two filmscripts, an original screenplay on which he is collaborating with James Ivory, and an adaptation of *A Pale View of Hills* for Japanese film production. Ishiguro enjoys alternating between the solitary, individualistic enterprise of novel writing and the collaborative, communal activity of film writing. He views the two as complementary artistic endeavors.

Critics have addressed the issue of Ishiguro's literary an-
cestry in a predictable way, assuming that Japanese writers must
have been of chief importance to him. From the evidence of the
fiction and interviews, however, this is not the case. Although it
is true that Japanese films, by the author's own admission, have
been influential, it is largely the "Western tradition"—and particularly nineteenth-century English and Russian writers such
as "Dostoevsky, Chekhov, Charlotte Bronte, Dickens"—that
stands behind Ishiguro's novelistic output.[13] Ishiguro's work also
betrays the influence of such modern novelists as E. M. Forster
(for his "plain" style of writing and for his interrogation of the
idea and ideal of England), Ford Madox Ford (for his vivid portrait of character and narrative repression), Henry James (for his
ability to show "us people changing their self-images—gradu-
ally, hesitantly, yet with lasting, troubling consequences")[14] and,
more recently, Franz Kafka (for his depictions of the uncanny).

For all of their obvious and significant differences, Ishiguro's
novels share many characteristics; there is a coherency and integrity to what Malcolm Bradbury calls Ishiguro's "aesthetic
invention."[15] As Ishiguro himself observes, his novels center on
protagonists—Etsuko, Ono, Stevens, and Ryder—whose "lives
are spoiled because they don't have any extraordinary insight
into life. They're not necessarily stupid, they're just ordinary."[16]
These characters are normal individuals who cannot see "beyond their immediate surroundings" and who are therefore "at
the mercy of what this world immediately around" them "proclaims itself to be."[17]

Further, the novels are each narrated in the first person by
protagonists who have something to hide, from themselves no

less than from their readers, yet who reconstruct their past failures and misplaced loyalties nostalgically, even elegiacally. Unsurprisingly, these first-person protagonists make for "unreliable" narrators—narrators, in Wayne Booth's influential term, who fail to speak for or act in accordance with the norms of the work, and who therefore are to be construed ironically in one way or another.[18] In this connection, what Ishiguro says of his first novel is germane to all of them: "the whole narrative strategy of the book was about how someone ends up talking about things they cannot face directly through other people's stories. I was trying to explore . . . how people use the language of self-deception and self-protection."[19] In another interview Ishiguro puts this even more baldly: "The language I use [in my novels] tends to be the sort that actually suppresses meaning and tries to hide away meaning. . . ."[20]

In a study of first-person narrators in fiction, David Goldknopf writes that I-narrators tend either to "haul us immediately into the narrative situation" through a "direct appeal for our attention," or to "intervene *between* us and the narrative situation, forcing us always to evaluate the latter *through*" them, "making the operation" of their minds "the true subject matter of the story."[21] Ishiguro's protagonist-narrators—Etsuko, Ono, Stevens, and Ryder—engage in both strategies simultaneously, insisting that their readers take them at their word yet conditioning these readers to second-guess their perceptions, to read between the lines of their narratives. Put another way, all of Ishiguro's narrators claim to be offering their readers accurate reconstructions of their pasts when in fact they "attempt to conceal the overbearing shame associated with this past."[22] In this sense, "the truth is revealed to us through the words of narrators who themselves largely fail to see it."[23]

Ishiguro's novels also share an investment in interior, psychological concerns. While Amit Chaudhuri is correct to point out that Ishiguro's first three novels are about "the shame of being on the wrong side of history,"[24] and while Meera Tamaya is right to deem historical events "the powerful absences which shape" Ishiguro's "characters and narratives,"[25] the author is more a novelist of the inner character than of the outer world. To be sure, these novels readily engage historical and political realities, but history and politics are explored primarily in order to plumb the depths and shallows of the characters' emotional and psychological landscapes and only secondarily to explore, say, World War Two, Japanese fascism, or the English class system. As Ishiguro himself remarks of the genesis of his novels, "I would look for moments in history that would best serve my purposes. . . . I was conscious that I wasn't so interested in history per se, that I was using British history or Japanese history to illustrate something that was preoccupying me."[26] What preoccupies the novelist is psychological defenses and the "emotional arena" most broadly construed: the "suppression of emotion,"[27] the idealization of the self, and the ways in which individuals, in T. S. Eliot's line in *The Waste Land,* self-protectively mix "memory and desire."[28] Ishiguro explains in an interview that "I'm not overwhelmingly interested in what really did happen. What's important is the emotional aspect, the . . . position the characters take up at different points in the story, and why they need to take up these positions."[29] The author explores the terrain most influentially mapped out by Sigmund Freud, whose anatomy of re-

pression does as much as anyone's to open up Ishiguro's psychologically charged works. Indeed, Ishiguro betrays a debt to
Freud when he remarks of his characters, "I'm not interested in
the solid facts" but "in the emotional upheaval"[30] or when he
notes his interest in "how one uses memory for one's own purposes, one's own ends."[31]

Ishiguro likes to follow his protagonists' "thoughts around,
as they try to trip themselves up or to hide from themselves."[32]
His protagonists employ one or more psychological defense
mechanisms—in particular, repression—to keep certain unwel-
come memories or intolerable desires at bay. Ishiguro's novels
focus on individuals who repress knowledge about their pasts in
order to protect themselves from painful experiences, or who
repress wishes that they cannot face or even admit—wishes that,
in Freud's phrase, prove to be "incompatible" with their "ethical
and aesthetic standards."[33] As Ishiguro himself comments of his
protagonists, they

> know what they have to avoid and that determines the
> routes they take through memory, and through the past.
> There's no coincidence that they're usually worrying over
> the past. They're worrying because they sense there isn't
> something quite right there. But of course memory is this
> terribly treacherous terrain, the very ambiguities of
> memory go to feed self-deception.[34]

Ishiguro's novels also eschew "plottiness" and worldly action in favor of a more interior focus ("I try to put in as little plot
as possible").[35] Even those Japanese films that Ishiguro most

admires avoid "anything that is overtly melodramatic or plotty" and try "to remain within the realms of everyday experience."[36] Ozu films and Chekhov plays and stories, Ishiguro recounts, have given him "the courage and conviction to have a very slow pace and not worry if there isn't a strong plot," to aspire to "slowness," with "things almost stopping."[37] Careful readers, however, will see that the stasis and quietness in the author's novels are superficial rather than deep. "There's a surface quietness to my books—there aren't a lot of people getting murdered or anything like that," Ishiguro observes. "But for me, they're not quiet books, because they're books that deal with things that disturb me the most and questions that worry me the most."[38] Indeed, what Salman Rushdie writes of *Remains of the Day* applies equally well to Ishiguro's other novels: "Just below the understatement of the novel's surface is a turbulence as immense as it is slow."[39]

Although his novels are experimental in a "quiet" way, Ishiguro attempts to avoid openly postmodern elements in his books; he seeks to avoid the trap of writing novels that can be taken as meditations on "the nature of fiction."[40] For Ishiguro, "the kind of book whose *raison d'etre* is to say something about literary form [is] very tedious. . . . I'm only interested in literary experiment insofar as it serves a purpose of exploring certain themes with an emotional dimension. I always try to disguise those elements of my writing that I feel perhaps are experimental."[41] "I don't believe that the nature of fiction is one of the burning issues of the late twentieth century," the author remarks; "It's not one of the things I want to turn to novels and art to find out about."[42] Rather, Ishiguro appears to be more interested in tackling and reworking his culture's dominant myths, in communicating a vision, and in exploring what "is perhaps the scariest arena in life," the "emotional arena."[43]

That Ishiguro's novels eschew a postmodern dimension does not make them simple or straightforward. In fact, their psychological and particularly their chronological complexity render them difficult and even opaque for novice readers. As one critic explains the difficulty, "in his novels Ishiguro reaches back and forth in time with later events prefiguring earlier events, so that even to a reader with a highly retentive memory who reads the book at one sitting the significance of what is earlier revealed is not available until a second reading on which the novel will read like a new novel about familiar people."[44] For this reason, what Joseph Frank has remarked of James Joyce is no less true of Ishiguro: he "cannot be read—he can only be reread."[45] It is only upon repeated encounters with and careful study of Ishiguro's fictions that these vague stories of seemingly mundane lives are revealed in all of their significance, clarity, and power.

CHAPTER TWO

A Pale View of Hills

Memory, I realize, can be an unreliable thing;
often it is heavily coloured by the circumstances in
which one remembers, and no doubt this applies to
certain of the recollections I have gathered here.

Etsuko,
in *A Pale View of Hills,* 156

A Pale View of Hills is a precocious first novel: subtly ironic, tightly structured, stylistically restrained—yet emotionally and psychologically explosive. As one reader puts it, *A Pale View of Hills* is remarkable for its "control and economy," which resemble "the work of a much more experienced writer."[1] Ishiguro's first novel is brief, elliptical, and spare; it works "largely by inference,"[2] leaving "more questions unanswered than answered."[3]

The novel concerns Etsuko, a middle-aged Japanese woman presently living in an English "country house" who is the narrative's first person; her younger daughter, Niki, the offspring of Etsuko's second marriage (to Sheringham, a now-deceased English journalist who covered Japanese affairs); and Keiko, Etsuko's first daughter, who has committed suicide and who was the offspring of Etsuko's earlier marriage (to the Japanese businessman Jiro Ogata). The narrative moves back and forth, via Etsuko's memory and daydreams, between the present and past and between England and Nagasaki. The present of the novel is set in Etsuko's rural English home just after Niki's five-day April visit from London, in the late seventies or early eighties. On the surface neither Etsuko nor Niki is much preoccupied with thoughts of Keiko, who some months back hanged herself in her rented room in Manchester,[4] while on a deeper level there is little else that concerns them, Keiko's death "hovering over" them whenever they talk (10). The "past" of the novel, narrated by Etsuko and comprising the majority of the book's pages, centers mainly upon several weeks of one summer in the late forties or early fifties in Etsuko's section of eastern Nagasaki, when World War Two was recently ended, when "there was fighting in Korea" (11), and when many people remained "shocked" by Nagasaki's nuclear devastation (58). During this same summer, significantly, Etsuko is pregnant with Keiko and expresses "misgivings about motherhood" (99).

Rounding out the reader's picture of Etsuko's immediate family are her memories of life early that summer with her first husband, Jiro, and with his visiting father, Seiji Ogata, a retired school teacher affectionately known as Ogata-San. Although it is never stated explicitly, the reader learns from these remembrances that Etsuko's marriage to Jiro was unhappy—that Jiro had time only for his work and newspaper, and that otherwise he either ignored or bullied his wife. The reader also learns that he is jokingly called "Pharaoh" at work for urging his underlings to "work like slaves while he does nothing himself" except read the newspaper (61)—behavior that approximates his treatment of Etsuko. Jiro's benign (and sometimes not so benign) neglect of his wife is also echoed in his lack of interest in and even hostility toward his visiting father, who years back introduced

Jiro to Etsuko. Indeed, Etsuko herself is far kinder and more attentive to the aging widower than is his own son, who is clearly only too happy to see his father's visit come to an end (154).

Like Etsuko, Ogata-San attempts to rationalize his wartime activities by relying upon a "foggy memory" (56) to help him explain away his professional conduct prior to and during the war. While somewhat peripheral in *A Pale View of Hills,* Ogata-San's obsession is taken up more fully in Ishiguro's second novel, *An Artist of the Floating World,* in the character of the novel's protagonist, Masuji Ono. Cynthia F. Wong writes that Ono's story in the later novel "is less a reflection of his glory days as an artist in Imperial Japan than a rationalizing account of his own participation in world affairs,"[5] which also serves as an apt description of Ogata-San's story. Ogata-San's visit with Jiro and Etsuko that summer, his "first visit since moving away from Nagasaki earlier that year" (28), follows a written attack on Ogata's wartime professional activities by an ex-friend of Jiro's and ex-student of Ogata's, Shigeo Matsuda, who has become a communist. Ogata wishes Jiro to respond to Shigeo's offending article on his behalf, on the grounds that it constitutes an "attack on the family name" (126). Clearly, the self-absorbed Jiro has no interest in taking up this cause, leaving Ogata to confront the author of the article alone. Specifically, Ogata is accused of helping to lead Japan in "a misguided direction, an evil direction"— into war—and of "sacking and imprisoning" five teachers with opposing views in April of 1938 (147–48). Ogata, by contrast, views himself as having made a "contribution" (150) to his nation, and defends his activities as rooted in a "deep" concern "for the country" and in a desire to see that "correct values" are "preserved and handed on" (147). In this way, Ogata anticipates not only Ono in *An Artist of the Floating World* but Stevens in *The Remains of the Day,* both of whom rationalize past "professional" failures through the defense mechanisms of repression and projection rather than own up to personal failure or poor judgment.

Even more significant than Etsuko's story of her immediate family that summer, however, is her story of a mother and daughter, Sachiko and Mariko, whom Etsuko befriends "towards the beginning" of that same summer, when Etsuko was in her "third or fourth month of pregnancy" (12). As Etsuko puts it of her relationship with Sachiko that summer, "for a short time . . . I was admitted into her confidence" (13), an event that parallels the reader's fleeting admission into Etsuko's confidence. Etsuko meets the thirty-ish Sachiko and her daughter of about ten years of age when they move into a shabby, unelectrified cottage situated across a barren field from Etsuko and Jiro's modern, postwar apartment complex. Before she moves into the cottage near Etsuko, Sachiko, who is originally from Tokyo, arrives in Nagasaki in order to live with her uncle, having lost her husband in the war (45). The parallels between Etsuko and Sachiko begin to mount up: just as Sachiko's uncle earlier took in a desperate Sachiko, so Ogata-San earlier took in a desperate Etsuko, who had lost her family, presumably to the bomb. And while never directly stated, Sachiko's past marriage, like Etsuko's present one, shows all the signs of wife abuse. Sachiko's husband was "very strict and very patriotic"; never "the most considerate of men," he forbade Sachiko to learn English, even forcing her to throw away her English books (110). Fumio

Yoshioka is right to observe in both marriages "an alarming disconnection of both verbal and spiritual communication."[6] These abusive relationships echo the one between Jiro's business underling, Hanada, and his wife, in which Hanada apparently threatened to beat his wife with a golf club because she would not vote the way he wanted her to during an election (62).

It also becomes evident that Etsuko is overcome with a painful past and sense of personal failure that she attempts, sometimes successfully and sometimes not, to repress: a phenomenon that will be treated in greater detail in the discussion of Stevens in *The Remains of the Day*. Indeed, Etsuko's "real" story is told exclusively by indirection. In the novel's first paragraph, for example, Etsuko admits her "selfish desire not to be reminded of the past" (9). Later, she admits that she has "no wish to ponder" again certain circumstances of her past (91), even though these circumstances are precisely what her narrative, at least indirectly, is all about. Like Etsuko's walk in the nearby Nakagawa district, her narrative itself reveals her "mixed emotions of sadness and pleasure" and her "deep sense of loss" (23). And just as Ogata-San at one point appears to Etsuko to be choosing a walking "route so as to deliberately avoid" his old haunts in Nagasaki (141), so Etsuko deliberately avoids mentioning Keiko's suicide to an acquaintance, Mrs. Waters, who inquires after Etsuko's elder daughter (50–51). Etsuko at one juncture puts it, "as with a wound on one's own body, it is possible to develop an intimacy with the most disturbing of things" (54), a comment that serves nicely as a gloss on her ability to repress the "real" tale within her ostensible one. Fumio Yoshioka comments of this passage, "When one scar is too fresh and too rugged to be examined scrutinizingly, its pain and heat could be conveyed by detailing another scar of the past, even though it belongs to someone else."[7] Also like Ogata-San, Etsuko excuses her own self-deception by hiding behind the inevitable inaccuracies of memory: "It is possible that my memory of these events will have grown hazy with time," she insists, "that things did not happen in quite the way they come back to me today" (41). The novel repeatedly alludes to the hidden meaning of Etsuko's narrative: just as a wound on Mariko's cheek turns out to be a smudge of mud (16), and just as people smile and laugh when they are sad and disappointed (131, 149), things are not as they at first appear to be in Etsuko's story of *another* woman's sacrifice of her daughter. Indeed, her narrative itself resembles the money she at one point offers Sachiko: both are "wrapped" in a "silk scarf of a suitably discrete pattern" (71). Or like Sachiko's cottage, much of which remains "in shadow," Etsuko's real story is a dimly lit one the reader must strain to make out. Like Etsuko's uncommunicative relationship with Jiro, all that is important in her narrative is expressed "by the way" and tacitly: "it was never in the nature of our relationship to discuss . . . things openly" (126–27). In this connection, it is instructive to note that the paleness in the novel's title alludes not to the distant hills themselves but to the faded view, dim perception, or distant memory of them. As Ishiguro himself puts it in an interview, *A Pale View of Hills,* as with all of his novels, is concerned less with "solid facts" than with "emotional upheaval," with "how one uses memory for one's own purposes, one's own ends."[8]

Related to Etsuko's suppression of memory is the fact that she fails to articulate the problem of Mariko's scarred upbringing at the hands of Sachiko, or that the child exhibits alarmingly reclusive, antisocial behavior. To invoke Henry James's distinction, she can only show, not tell, it. Sachiko's abuse of Mariko takes many forms. For example, she allows her daughter to remain out of school (20), justifying it because of "one thing or another, and our moving around so much" (45); allows her to fight freely with other children (14–15); strikes her (85); and leaves her unattended for long stretches of time—even at night during a period of mysterious "child murders" (100). Sachiko is only too happy to leave her daughter with Etsuko, at that time a virtual stranger, for an entire day (15), rationalizing her negligence by arguing, in effect, that past neglect excuses present neglect: "Mariko should be capable of being left on her own by now" (73). As Peter Wain observes, Sachiko's "relationship with her daughter is at best negligent and possibly even murderous."[9] The pregnant Etsuko attempts to mitigate this abuse by volunteering to take care of Mariko and by helping to search for her when she is missing (36–37); by arranging for a job for Sachiko; and even by volunteering personal funds to alleviate Sachiko's, and hence Mariko's, material deprivation.

The most disturbing of all of Sachiko's forms of neglect, however, is when she leaves Mariko unattended for hours in order to fraternize with Frank, an American soldier ("American soldiers were as numerous as ever" in Japan at that time [11]) whom Sachiko befriends and who promises to remove her from her squalid and constraining circumstances. This twist of the plot clues the reader into one of the novel's primary intertexts, James Joyce's "Eveline" from *Dubliners*. Joyce's short story concerns the escape fantasy of Eveline Hill, a young woman

who dreams of transcending her dreary, impoverished, stultify-
ing Dublin existence, with its imprisoning family obligations, in
order to set sail with Frank, a sailor who has known "distant
countries,"[10] for exotic Argentina. Working against Eveline's
realization of this escape fantasy is her promise to her now-deceased mother that she will "keep the home together,"[11] includ-
ing taking care of her aging and frequently drunken, abusive
father. In contrast to a drab and grinding reality, Eveline now
imagines herself "about to explore another life with Frank. Frank
was very kind, manly, open-hearted. She was to go away with
him by the night-boat to be his wife and to live with him in
Buenos Ayres where he had a home waiting for her."[12] Feeling
that "her time was running out,"[13] Eveline conjures an escape
fantasy—by definition a "quick fix" at little cost—that the reader
quickly senses is doomed to failure: "She stood up in a sudden
impulse of terror. Escape! She must escape! Frank would save
her. He would give her life, perhaps love, too. But she wanted to
live. Why should she be unhappy? She had a right to happiness.
Frank would take her in his arms, fold her in his arms. He would
save her."[14]

Like Eveline's would-be rescuer, Sachiko's too is named
Frank—an ironic choice in both cases in that neither man appears to be frank about following through with his promises.
Indeed, in each case it appears that Frank's intention is to seduce
and abandon his desperate female victim. Sachiko too is to leave
by ship with her Frank—for America via Kobe (46, 163). She
too clearly dreams of escaping her familial responsibility, in this
case the care of her daughter, Mariko. And Sachiko too seeks to
escape her straightened financial situation ("You have no idea,

Etsuko, how relieved I'll be to leave this place. I trust I've seen the last of such squalor" [164]) for a life of prestige, wealth, adventure, and romance. "When I was young, " Sachiko admits to Etsuko, "I used to dream I'd go to America one day, that I'd go there to become a film actress" (109). Moreover, neither Eveline's father nor Sachiko's daughter remotely likes the Frank in question; and both Eveline and Sachiko are persuaded to stick with their Franks, no matter how unlikely these men are to follow through with their commitments: "Could she still draw back after all he had done for her?"[15] "Why would he have gone to all this trouble if he wasn't absolutely sincere? Why would he have gone to all this trouble on my behalf?" (169–70). Of course, despite all of these similarities, Eveline's and Sachiko's situations resolve themselves differently: Eveline, at the last moment, refuses to leave Dublin, betraying a paralyzing guilt and pathetic self-victimization; while Sachiko is only too willing to leave Japan, despite her recognition that Frank may well abandon her and her daughter, as he has done once before (68–69, 169–70). In any case, it becomes clear that Sachiko "is sure to be betrayed,"[16] though it is never divulged precisely what becomes of her. And Sachiko's behavior proves to be more reprehensible than Eveline's on at least one other score: she abandons her daughter in order to carry on with a man in a bar (40)—a man who, earlier, "disappeared and spent all [of Sachiko's] money, drank it all in three days" (87). Although Sachiko repeatedly insists that "what is of utmost importance to me is my daughter's welfare"—that "I'm not some young saloon girl with no regard for decency" (86)—she nevertheless continually and troublingly changes her mind as to whether it is in her daughter's best interest to remain in Japan or to make the move to America (44, 46, 68–69, 86–87, 102, 170), leaving Etsuko (and the reader) suspicious of her true motivations. Ishiguro's Frank is not only reminiscent of Joyce's Frank but of Puccini's Benjamin Franklin Pinkerton, from *Madame Butterfly,* an American naval officer who seduces and abandons the Japanese female protagonist of the opera.

There is one more major surprise in Etsuko's narrative that the reader discovers by the end of the novel: that Sachiko and Mariko function less as "real" individuals than as individuals onto whom Etsuko can project her own guilt for neglecting and abusing Keiko. Clearly, Etsuko fears that this neglect precipitated her first daughter's suicide. While many readers have simply assumed that Sachiko and Mariko are "real people" in Etsuko's life, it is probably the case that Sachiko, like Mariko's mysterious woman visitor, is neither exactly as she appears to be nor "entirely imaginary" (43), but something in between— the product of what Ishiguro in an interview calls a "highly Etsuko-ed version" of Sachiko's story. Because, Ishiguro explains, "it's really Etsuko talking about herself," the "meanings that Etsuko imputes to the life of Sachiko are obviously the meanings that are relevant" to Etsuko's own life. "Whatever the facts were about what happened to Sachiko and her daughter, they are of interest to Etsuko now because she can use them to talk about herself."[17] Or as Fumio Yoshioka puts it, Sachiko and Mariko function as alter egos of "the heroine and Keiko respectively."[18]

Hints abound to suggest that Etsuko's narrative of Sachiko's treatment of Mariko is a coded way for her to comment on her own treatment of Keiko, that Sachiko's story is closer to Etsuko's than the latter would have the reader believe. Not only are Keiko and Mariko immediately conjoined in Etsuko's thinking (11), but Etsuko identifies with Sachiko's aloofness (13); Sachiko makes Etsuko "laugh self-consciously" (15); and Mariko makes Etsuko "experience a curious feeling of unease" (16). Moreover, Etsuko's defensiveness about leaving Japan uncannily mirrors Sachiko's: "But such things are long in the past now and I have no reason to ponder them yet again. My motives for leaving Japan were justifiable, and I know I always kept Keiko's interests very much at heart. There is nothing to be gained from going over such matters again" (91). And when Sachiko, in the presence of Etsuko, insists that it is in her own best interest to leave Japan, she then adds tellingly, "You know that yourself, Etsuko" (170–71).

A final hint that Etsuko's narrative of Sachiko's motherhood is a way of talking about her own anxiety, depression, and feelings of inadequacy regarding her then-impending motherhood arises when Etsuko admits that just about anything at that time was "capable of arousing in me every kind of misgiving about motherhood" (17). Otherwise, Etsuko's fear of parenthood (112) is gauged only indirectly, through others. At points, for example, Mrs. Fujiwara reveals that Etsuko appears "unhappy" (77) and "miserable" (24). She then attempts to reassure her: "Once the child comes . . . you'll be delighted, believe me" (77). A mother, she also cautions her, "needs a positive attitude to bring up a child" (24–25). Etsuko's sense of foreboding about motherhood is also suggested when she insists upon her present state of happiness with Jiro and with her pregnancy in the same breath (34, 46), leading readers to wonder whether she is happy with either situation. More to the point, Etsuko may only be pretending "to be delighted" that a child is on the way (49); instead, like Frank, she may actually be "scared of" the child (86). Even Sachiko's and Mrs. Fujiwara's repeated assurances that Etsuko will "make a splendid mother" (14, 15, 77) fail to allay, and instead only intensify, her fears. Niki expresses similar misgivings about motherhood when she exclaims to Etsuko, "I don't want to just get stuck away somewhere with a husband and a load of screaming kids" (180).

Toward the end of the novel, in one of its dramatic climaxes, Etsuko abruptly drops the pretense that Sachiko's tale and her own are two entirely different narratives. This is when, as Ishiguro explains, the truth "slips out: she's now talking about herself. She's no longer bothering to put it in the third person."[19] In effect, this dramatic scene between Etsuko and Mariko dissolves into one between Etsuko and Keiko: it is now Etsuko who promises her own daughter that if things do not work out "over there, we'll come straight back" (172–73); it is now Etsuko who is the mother guilty of negligent child rearing; it is now Etsuko who, as she later admits to Niki, "knew all along" that Keiko "wouldn't be happy over here. But I decided to bring her just the same" (176). But Etsuko's admission of guilt is quickly followed by her insistence that she and Niki "not discuss it any further," that "there's no point in going over all that now" (176). Ironically, the entire story has been discussed and gone over by other means: via Etsuko's repressed, projected, and rationalized tale of Sachiko and Mariko.

In an interview, Ishiguro discusses the way Etsuko uses her own narrative. She "talks around" what is really bothering her,

employing a "language of self-deception and self-protection.
. . . Instead, she tells another story altogether, going back years
and talking about somebody she once knew. So the whole narrative strategy of the book [is] about how someone ends up talking about things they cannot face directly through other people's
stories."[20] Ishiguro here alludes to projection and rationalization, both of which, like repression, are defense mechanisms of
the ego. Such defense mechanisms allow the individual in question to transfer feelings of personal guilt to the external world.
As Calvin S. Hall explains, "A person who is afraid of his own
aggressive . . . impulses obtains some relief for his anxiety by
attributing aggressiveness . . . to other people. They are the ones
who are aggressive . . . not he."[21] In this connection, Etsuko is
clearly guilty of scapegoating—of using her "Sachiko narrative"
to deflect her personal guilt onto another. It is not she who has
"sacrificed" a daughter, who is guilty, figuratively speaking, of
infanticide, but someone else. Like Ogata-San, who imagines
his own disappointment with his son's actions as Etsuko's disappointment (131–32), Etsuko projects her past difficulties with
Keiko onto Sachiko/Mariko. "Of course," Hall writes, "the
whole affair is an elaborate subterfuge or rationalization for
evading personal responsibility for one's acts by blaming someone else"[22]—which is precisely Etsuko's unconscious intention.
By projecting her guilt onto Sachiko, Etsuko attempts to "avoid
punishment and self-blame by inventing plausible excuses and
alibis" for her misdeeds. She is, in effect, "rewarded for distort-
ing the truth."[23] The outcome of all of this, in Gabriele Annan's
words, is that "Ishiguro puts across Etsuko's inadequacy behind her back. . . ."[24]

Etsuko also engages in rationalization. Indeed, Niki, Etsuko's younger daughter, functions chiefly as Etsuko's rationalizing voice, explaining away the fact that Etsuko deserted her first daughter. "So many women," Niki tells Etsuko, "get stuck with kids and lousy husbands and they're just miserable. But they can't pluck up the courage to do anything about it. They'll just go on like that for the rest of their lives. . . . It couldn't have been easy, what you did, mother. You ought to be proud of what you did with your life" (89–90). And later Niki adds: "And you did everything you could for [Keiko]. You're the last person anyone could blame" (176). This is precisely what Etsuko herself would like to believe but cannot, her guilt for removing Keiko from Japan being anything but absolved.

That Etsuko and Niki experience unabated guilt for Keiko's suicide is made clear in their never-articulated fear that Keiko's ghost haunts her old room in Etsuko's English country house. The reason for Etsuko's buried guilt is obvious. Niki's unsettled conscience, on the other hand, is less easily explained, though it may be attributed both to "survivor's guilt" and to the fact that she purposefully absented herself from her sister's funeral. At one point Niki abruptly announces that she would like to sleep in a bedroom other than her old one, it being "right opposite" Keiko's old room. Etsuko too experiences "a disturbing feeling about that room opposite. . . . In many ways, that room is the most pleasant in the house, with a splendid view across the orchard. But it had been Keiko's fanatically guarded domain for so long, a strange spell seemed to linger there even now, six years after she had left it—a spell that had grown all the stronger now that Keiko was dead" (53). And in the early morning hours of the fifth day of Niki's visit, Etsuko believes that she hears "a small sound, some movement from within Keiko's room." Upon inspecting the room she sees nothing yet "feels the cold" (88–89). Niki also hears a noise, not being able to "sleep properly," but then nervously attributes it to Etsuko's movements, not to Keiko's (94–95). Perhaps for this reason Gabriele Annan deems *A Pale View of Hills* a "ghost story."[25]

Etsuko and Niki also suffer from bad dreams, which further suggests their feelings of lingering culpability. While Etsuko's dream of the little girl she has seen swinging in the park the previous day at first seems "perfectly innocent" (47), she later realizes, after its recurrence, that "the dream had to do not so much with the little girl we had watched, but with my having remembered Sachiko two days previously" (55). Like Niki herself, the reader is by now suspicious that this realization itself is an "innocent" interpretation of what the dream really concerns. For clearly, although Etsuko denies it, the dream concerns Keiko (95); and the little girl in the dream is not "on a swing at all" (96) but instead hangs from the end of a noose.

The novel's recurring nightmare and ghost motifs, which imply that Etsuko and Niki cannot live down or directly address their guilt, intertwine late in the novel, when Etsuko, early one morning, reports that she has "heard a sound come from within Keiko's room, a small clear sound," only to discover that the noise is being made by Niki, who is making coffee in the kitchen, and who claims to be sleepless from a night of "bad dreams" that are clearly, despite her denials, all about Keiko (174–75). As Etsuko puts it, while Etsuko and Niki "never dwelt long on the subject of Keiko's death, it was never far away, hovering

A PALE VIEW OF HILLS

over us whenever we talked" (10). And as Ishiguro himself contends, *A Pale View of Hills* "is largely based around [Etsuko's] guilt. She feels a great guilt" for sacrificing "her first daughter's happiness."[26] On the other hand, these mothers—as well as their daughters—are sacrificial victims of a rigid patriarchy that uses and then abandons them, leaving them to carry on as best they can.

But the novel works on an even deeper, more resonant level, one rooted both in the ancient Greek myth of Styx and in modern psychology. On the first score, Styx allusions contribute significantly to Ishiguro's depiction of his novel's terrain and personages, and to the narrative's symbolic depth. In Greek mythology Styx is both "the main river of Hades" and "its goddess." "The waters of the Styx were fatal to life, so that 'crossing the Styx' meant death and was to be feared and abhorred."[27] Taken together with the fact that the Styx's waters are said to be muddy,[28] this allusion nicely illuminates the deathly "expanse of wasteground, practically on the edge of the river" (12), that runs near Sachiko's and Etsuko's places of residence near Nagasaki. Indeed, this no-man's-land, with its mysterious, muddy river, is figured in the novel as a gulf between the living and the dead: "Between us and the river lay an expanse of wasteground, several acres of dried mud and ditches. Many complained it was a health hazard, and indeed the drainage was appalling. All year round there were craters filled in with stagnant water, and in the summer months the mosquitoes became intolerable" (11). Moreover, the reeds that grow along the water's edge are said to "cast long shadows on the muddy ground" (166–67), and the "journey" across the wasteground is described as "loathsome" (99).

This river is repeatedly figured as a doorway into another realm. Etsuko, for example, tells Sachiko that "the river's quite dangerous in places" (15), and therefore that the two of them should seek out the missing Mariko lest she be crossing the river bridge to "other side," to the "other bank," to wander in its dark, unexplored woods: "That was the first time I had crossed to the far side of the river. The ground felt soft, almost marshy under my feet. Perhaps it is just my fancy that I felt a cold touch of unease there on that bank, a feeling not unlike premonition, which caused me to walk with renewed urgency towards the darkness of the trees before us" (39–40). Moreover, when Etsuko and Sachiko find Mariko on the other side of the river she is figured as if dead—as having crossed the Styx, with its "cold touch":

> I could see a short way along the bank something like a bundle lying on the grass, close to the river's edge. It was just discernible in the gloom, a few shades darker than the ground around it. . . . I remember with some distinctness that eerie spell which seemed to bind the two of us as we stood there in the coming darkness looking towards that shape further down the bank. . . . As we came nearer, I saw Mariko lying curled on her side, knees hunched, her back towards us. . . . Mariko's eyes were open and at first I thought she was dead. . . . Sachiko too was silent, examining her daughter, turning her in her arms as if she were a fragile, but senseless doll. (40–41)

Even Sachiko's unelectrified cottage, with its tomblike coolness, darkness, and shadow, its "stark shabbiness," and its "faint odour of dampness" (17–18), is figured as a meeting point between the two realms that Styx divides.

The river goddess Styx is also figured in *A Pale View of Hills:* in the deathly woman, who resembles a grim reaper, that Mariko fears "might come again" (80) and take her across the river. Although Etsuko and Sachiko claim that no one lives there—"It's just trees and forest over there"—Mariko repeatedly insists upon the existence of a "woman from across the river" who will "take me to her house: . . . The woman from across the river. She was here last night. While mother was away. . . . She said she'd take me to her house, but I didn't go with her. Because it was dark" (18–19). Later, Mariko insists that "The woman came round again" and "said she'd take me to her house" (27–28), uniting the novel's Styx allusion and the young Mariko's fear of death. Although the original "mysterious woman" whom Mariko encounters is now dead, having taken her own life after drowning her baby on the streets of Tokyo following a bombing (73–74), Etsuko later believes that she too sees this woman— who seems neither absolutely real nor "entirely imaginary" (43)—who for so long has frightened Mariko:

> I saw the figure walking across the wasteground towards the cottage. . . . It was a woman—a thin figure—and she walked with a slow deliberate step. . . . Her face was thin, and had a chalky paleness about it which at first quite unnerved me. She looked to be around seventy or so. . . . Her kimono was of a dark sombre colour, the kind normally worn in mourning. Her eyes were slightly hooded and watched me with no apparent emotion. (157–58)

When it becomes clear that the real woman behind the Styx figure Etsuko sees is only Sachiko's aged cousin—Yasuko Kawanda, who arrives at Sachiko's hut in funeral garb (having, appropriately, just come from a funeral), and who "cuts a figure as a messenger of death"[29]—it only reinforces the potency of the Styx imagery in the novel.

It is the characters' attraction to this river and to death, however, that suggests the novel's debt to modern psychoanalytic theory as well as to ancient myth. At points, for Mariko, Etsuko, and, apparently, Keiko, death is less a domain to be feared than a realm to be sought out. This attraction to the river (and figuratively, to suicide) first becomes evident when Etsuko admits to "finding it strangely peaceful to walk beside the river" (83). Later, she describes in detail the sensation she has when crossing over the river bridge: "While crossing it, I stopped for a moment to gaze at the evening sky. As I recall, a strange sense of tranquility came over me there on that bridge. I stood there for some minutes, leaning over the rail, listening to the sounds of the river below me. When finally I turned, I saw my own shadow, cast by the lantern, thrown across the wooden slats of the bridge" (172). In these passages, crossing over the mysterious river—figured as crossing over into another realm—is depicted by Etsuko as strangely peaceful, tranquil, and inviting, just as death apparently becomes to Keiko, who takes her own life. Similarly, Mariko appears to find death both a threat (she fears the mysterious "woman" [27–8]) and a state to be sought out (she frequently escapes to the river [79–80]). Although Mariko at first appears to be unaffected by witnessing the woman drowning her baby in Tokyo, she later becomes both confused by and obsessed with this woman, and has difficulty, like Etsuko and Sachiko, determining where her "fantasies begin and end" (75). She is traumatized by this event (73–74), and hence comes both to fear and to be drawn masochistically to the "woman" she believes is waiting for her in the dark forest on the other side of the river. As Etsuko observes, "Nothing you learn at that [young] age is totally lost" (52).

Freudian theory helps explain Mariko's (and Keiko's) attraction to the river (and hence, symbolically, to death). Freud postulates the existence of a death-wish, a sado-masochistic urge to self-destruction, that is triggered when an individual's aggression cannot find satisfactory outlet in the external world. When this happens the aggression is turned inward, increasing "the amount of self-destructiveness holding sway in the interior."[30] This phenomenon goes a long way toward explaining Mariko's and Keiko's aggressiveness toward themselves and their mothers.

Masochism is the taking of pleasure in pain (sadism, of course, is the taking of pleasure in the pain of others); it is rooted in the "need for punishment at the hands of a parental power."[31] In order to provoke punishment from the parents, "the masochist must do what is inexpedient, must act against his own interests . . . and must . . . destroy his own real existence."[32] This dynamic squarely addresses Sachiko's and Mariko's troubled relationship. Indeed, it is not merely coincidental that Sachiko's and Mariko's initials (S and M) hint at this very dynamic.

The psychoanalytic view of suicide—the ultimate act of masochism, yet one with sadistic implications as well—is also of relevance to Mariko's (and Keiko's) situation. Freud views suicide as "the fulfilment of a punishment (self-punishment), and the fulfilment of a wish." No one, he adds, "finds the mental energy required to kill himself unless, in the first place, in doing so he is at the same time killing an object with whom he has identified himself, and, in the second place, is turning against himself a death-wish which had been directed against someone else."[33]

In this light, Mariko's symbolic suicide (40–41), which presages Keiko's actual one, reflects Mariko's frustrated desire to murder her abusive and neglectful, murderously self-absorbed mother. Sachiko's "murderous" intentions toward Mariko are most clearly revealed in Sachiko's treatment of Mariko's young cats, the young girl's only friends and love-objects. Indeed, in a larger sense Sachiko's treatment of Mariko's cats is a figuration of her treatment of Mariko (kittens are repeatedly linked with children in this novel), and the behavior of both toward the animals and toward each other reveals not only Sachiko's sadism but Mariko's masochism. For example, although it is made clear that there is plenty of room for these cats (and for Mariko) at Sachiko's uncle's house (162), Sachiko nevertheless refuses to oblige her daughter, and insists that when they leave Japan the cats will need to be given away, drowned, or abandoned. At one point Sachiko claims that "we'll just have to leave" the cats in Japan (164), and at another she insists that "we'll have to drown them" (84). Moreover, it is hinted that Sachiko, months earlier in Tokyo, disposed of one of Mariko's cats: "She disappeared. The day before we were leaving" (81). And it is repeatedly made clear that the young cats symbolize a young Mariko. Mariko's cat is a "stray," just as Mariko is something of a stray child ("The place is alive with stray cats," Sachiko at one point tellingly exclaims; "I'm not so optimistic about these kittens" [19]); and Sachiko hits both the cats and her child with apparent abandon (she slaps Mariko "sharply on the back of her thigh" [85], just as she gives a kitten "a sharp slap with the back of her hand" [47]). The clearest link between the cats and Mariko comes when Sachiko, in exasperation, attempts to take the kittens away from Mariko so that she can dispose of them before the two leave Japan. Sachiko chides Mariko:

> Aren't you old enough yet to see there are other things besides these filthy little animals? You'll just have to grow up a little. You simply can't have these sentimental attachments forever. These are just . . . just *animals* don't you see? . . . What does it matter about the dirty little creatures? . . . Why can't you understand that, Mariko? *Are you really too young? It's not your little baby, it's just an animal.* . . . (165, emphasis added)

Indeed, the connection here is more explicit than implicit: Sachiko treats Mariko less like her "baby" than like a "filthy little" animal or a "dirty little" creature worthy only of abandonment or worse.

Sachiko's figurative murder of her daughter takes place in this overdetermined first climax of the novel, when the Styx-like muddy river becomes a literal place of death for the cats. Sachiko takes Mariko's kittens down to the river to drown them, mirroring two previous events: the drowning of the child in Tokyo and the mysterious child murders then raging in Nagasaki.

Rather than simply letting the cats "loose"—"You never know,"
Etsuko observes reasonably, "someone may want them"—
Sachiko insists upon drowning them. This episode reveals a sa-
domasochistic moment between mother and daughter: Sachiko
knows that Mariko, "standing several yards behind her," is ob-
serving her drown the kittens. Rather than stop, however, Sachiko
merely throws "a glance over her shoulder towards her daughter," whom she notes is "watching" it all. Sachiko then continues to hold the cat under water, in what is clearly a symbolic act
of child murder. That Mariko insists upon watching the grue-
some goings-on suggests a masochistic impulse, that she takes
pleasure in her own pain. Sachiko is finally successful in drowning the cats by putting them in a vegetable box (that was supposed to have housed, not to have destroyed, the cats) and then
by sinking the entire thing in the river—right before Mariko's
"blank" gaze (166–68).

Sachiko's symbolic murder of Mariko appears to have nothing to do with Etsuko and Keiko until the reader recalls Etsuko's
treatment of the "young tomato plants" growing in the garden of
her English country house, which she has all but intentionally
"ruined." Admitting that "I've really rather neglected them"
(91)—that "I really have been rather neglectful about those tomatoes this year. . . . Still, it doesn't really matter, I suppose. I
never know what to do with so many tomatoes these days" (92)—
Etsuko, it is hinted, has treated Keiko much as she has treated
her tomato plants and much as Sachiko has treated Mariko and
her cats. Etsuko neglects the young plants to the point of killing
them, and then dismisses it all by exclaiming, "it doesn't really
matter," closely echoing Sachiko's rhetoric about Mariko's cats.

It is in the second of the novel's two dramatic climaxes, however, where a final fear of Etsuko's is revealed: that she is, figuratively speaking, the murderer of Keiko. This fear is divulged through a series of associated images or events: Mariko climbs trees (118); Etsuko dreams about a girl hanging from a swing/noose (96); a particularly disturbing child murder occurs that summer, "The tragedy of the little girl found hanging from a tree" (156); and Etsuko is haunted by an image of Keiko hanging in her room in Manchester (54). Together, these images fuse into the "unpleasant image" (156) of Etsuko's complicity in Keiko's death. At one point, for example, while pursuing Mariko when she has run down to the river, Etsuko gets "an old piece of rope" tangled around her ankle—a rope the reader associates with Keiko's noose—that she removes and then holds in her hands shortly before catching up with the girl. Mariko becomes frightened, clearly believing that Etsuko is planning to use the rope to hang her, and with "signs of fear . . . appearing on her face," repeatedly asks, "Why have you got the rope?" (83–84). Still later in the novel, just before it becomes clear that Etsuko is speaking not to Mariko but to Keiko about leaving Japan, Mariko looks at Etsuko questioningly and watches her closely:

> "Why are you holding that [rope]?" she asked.
> "This? It just caught around my sandal, that's all."
> "Why are you holding it?"
> "I told you. It caught around my foot. . . . Why are you looking at me like that? I'm not going to hurt you." (173)

Etsuko's worst nightmare is glimpsed in this moment: that

she is somehow not merely loosely implicated in her first daughter's suicide but is its instigator. In this connection, when Etsuko says to Mariko/Keiko, "Everyone's a little frightened of new things. You'll like it over there" (173), "over there" may refer either to England/America or to death, to the other side of the river. In all of these ways, then, Etsuko's narrative, which superficially appears to be calm, even mundane, is revealed to be explosive and disturbing, exhibiting the taboo of infanticide at its very core. In this light, what Salman Rushdie concludes of *The Remains of the Day* is doubly true of *A Pale View of Hills:* "Just below the understatement of the novel's surface is a turbulence as immense as it is slow."[34]

Although Cynthia F. Wong is certainly correct to point out that *A Pale View Of Hills* concerns the nuclear devastation of postwar Nagasaki, then, she nevertheless may overstate the case when she argues that "What begins for Etsuko as a personal post-mortem, inquiring into her daughter's death, evolves into a tale about Nagasaki after the bombing."[35] Similarly, Edith Milton may go too far when she asserts that "Sachiko and Etsuko become minor figures in a greater pattern of betrayal, infanticide and survival played out against the background of Nagasaki, itself the absolute emblem of our genius for destruction."[36] Rather, Fumio Yoshioka strikes the appropriate balance when he remarks that "the focus of depiction is fixed on people and not on the horrendous incidents; on the devastated minds and lives of the survivors and not on the colossal devastation of the war and the atomic bomb."[37] Indeed, the focus of Ishiguro's first novel is more on individual psychology—specifically, on the way in which people use other people's stories to conceal yet, paradoxi-

A PALE VIEW OF HILLS

cally, to reveal their own—than it is on national history and the role individuals play in public affairs. This latter concern, however, would come to take center stage in Kazuo Ishiguro's second novel, *An Artist of the Floating World.*

CHAPTER THREE

An Artist of the Floating World

I cannot recall any colleague who could paint a
self-portrait with absolute honesty; however
accurately one may fill in the surface details of
one's mirror reflection, the personality represented
rarely comes near the truth as others would see it.

Ono,
in *An Artist of the Floating World,* 67

I'm interested in this business of values and ideals
being tested, and people having to face up to the
notion that their ideals weren't quite what they
thought they were before the test came.

Ishiguro,
in Swift, "Kazuo Ishiguro," 22

In many respects, *An Artist of the Floating World* continues
and develops the project Kazuo Ishiguro commenced in *A Pale
View of Hills.* The author's comparatively hopeful second novel,
however, focuses more directly on the relationship between private, psychological and worldly, political affairs than does his
first. As Nigel Hunt astutely observes, *An Artist* "concerns itself
with the influence and responsibility of the artist to society as
well as the way in which the present changes our perceptions of

AN ARTIST OF THE FLOATING WORLD

the past."[1] The novel centers on Masuji Ono, a Japanese artist now in his declining years, who looks back over his long life and career from the perspective of twenty months—between October, 1948, and June, 1950—that constitute the "present" of the novel. Although Ono is in many ways a fully fleshed-out version of Ogata-San in Ishiguro's earlier novel—both are former artists and art teachers, former fascists, and aging widowers who have children whose political views contrast sharply with their own—it is unfair to dismiss *Pale View,* as some have done, as merely "a trial run" for *An Artist.*[2] Indeed, for all of their similarities, the most striking of which is that both novels are narrated in the first person by protagonists who look back, elegiacally, nostalgically, and dishonestly, at their "failed" former lives, the later novel is a more optimistic one than Ishiguro's first: Ono moves closer than any other Ishiguro protagonist to admitting past mistakes and false "ideals." What this novel does share with the earlier book is its penetrating subtlety and quiet force—its surface calm and tempestuous depths—that stretch "the reader's awareness," teaching him or her how "to read more perceptively."[3]

Set in a provincial Japanese town, to which Ono first moves in 1913, the novel traces the protagonist's life, focusing on his artistic apprenticeship, fame (which peaks in 1938), and postwar decline. When the novel opens, in October of 1948, Ono's wife and only son are dead—victims of Japan's involvement in World War Two—and he is left with two daughters: the elder Setsuko, who is in her late twenties, married, and already a mother; and the younger Noriko, who is single and in her mid-twenties, and with whom Ono lives. Past events of Ono's long life are told as digressions from the "present" narrative, which superficially concerns his efforts to remove obstacles to Noriko's marriage, but which actually concerns these past events themselves or, more accurately, Ono's biased reconstruction and filtered understanding of them. As Cynthia F. Wong puts it, "Ono's tale is less a reflection of his glory days as an artist in Imperial Japan than a rationalizing account of his own participation in world affairs."[4]

Also like *Pale View, An Artist* benefits from a focus on its protagonist's psychological state and understanding of the past. For in addition to prostituting his art to the imperialistic, militaristic aims of the Japanese emperor in the years leading up to and during World War Two, Ono is indirectly accountable for the deaths of his son, Kenji, and wife, Michiko. He is also accountable for the difficult time Noriko is now having concluding a marriage agreement. As Patrick Parrinder characterizes the latter crisis, "Now, as he tries to marry off his daughter, Ono's prestige as a former Fascist painter is a rapidly dwindling asset."[5] At one point Setsuko uncharacteristically faults Ono on this account, requesting that he "take certain precautionary steps" to ensure that such "misunderstandings" about the past do not arise again.[6] That Ono is indirectly to blame for the deaths of his wife, in a "freak raid" at the war's end (91), and son, in a battle, is suggested by Setsuko's husband, Suichi, who hints that men like Ono "led the country astray," resulting in actions like Ono's son "attempting that hopeless charge across the minefield" (56–57), the apotheosis of futile, self-destructive action.

Ono's daughters worry that his shame will lead him to commit suicide, an act then considered to be an honorable way of apologizing for involving Japan in an unjust and losing battle. Indeed, a composer of patriotic songs and a major corporate leader join the ranks of those recently taking their lives out of a sense of personal complicity. Ono, however, apparently never considers suicide; he feels less guilt over his past actions than his daughters imagine.

The large gap between Japan's postwar mentality, which Ono dismisses as cynical and bitter (21, 23), and Ono's retrograde nostalgia surfaces in the novel's numerous references to intergenerational tensions and to the postwar Americanization of Japan. The novel is fraught with what Patrick Parrinder calls the "mutual incomprehensions of the old and the young."[7] For example, not only does Ono's grandson Ichiro lack his mother's respect for and fear of the older generation (31), but this grandson adopts the American Lone Ranger and Popeye the Sailorman as his heroes, eschewing popular Japanese figures such as Lord Yoshitsune or Samurai warriors (30, 152). As Suichi puts the prevailing sentiment, "the American heroes are the better models for children now": it is more appropriate that Ichiro admire "cowboys than that he idolize people like Miyamoto Musashi" (36). Ono explains Suichi's sentiment away as so much unwarranted bitterness against the older generation (50). Yet the same sentiment is echoed by the man who eventually marries Noriko: "By and large," he claims, "the Americans have an immense amount to teach us" about "democracy and individual rights" (185).

By the end of the novel, in June of 1950, the reader learns that Noriko is married and expecting her first child; that Setsuko is now expecting her second child; and that Ono himself, who now walks with a cane, has suffered a significant illness (197–98)—one that leaves him more infirm than ever and that further diminishes his past "triumphs."

An Artist of the Floating World opens and closes with, and periodically returns to, Ono's mention of the "Bridge of Hesitation" (7, 204–5), linking this novel with its predecessor, which also prominently featured a bridge. "Hesitation" nicely sums up Ono's present mental state. "On three or four evenings a week," he recounts,

> I still find myself taking that path down to the river and the little wooden bridge still known to some who lived here before the war as 'the Bridge of Hesitation.' . . .
>
> We called it that because until not so long ago, crossing it would have taken you into our pleasure district, and conscience-troubled men—so it was said—were to be seen hovering there, caught between seeking an evening's entertainment and returning home to their wives. But if sometimes I am to be seen up on that bridge, leaning thoughtfully against the rail, it is not that I am hesitating. It is simply that I enjoy standing there as the sun sets, surveying my surroundings and the changes taking place around me. (99)

This passage figures Ono's present psychological predicament: he is a "conscience-troubled" man, though he would deny it, who hesitates between owning up to his past mistakes and covering them up; between moral responsibility and psychological expedience; between uncovering and further hiding his lingering guilt. Hence, Patrick Parrinder has merely taken Ono's bait when he describes the novel as a series of "rambling reminiscences of a retired painter."[8] Rather, Ono's "drifting" (48) and "digressing" (28) narrative is carefully designed to conceal while appearing to reveal his past culpability. This narrative duplicity can be glimpsed when Ono insists,

> I find it hard to understand how any man who values his self-respect would wish for long to avoid responsibility for his past deeds; it may not always be an easy thing, but there is certainly a satisfaction and dignity to be gained in coming to terms with the mistakes one has made in the course of one's life. In any case, there is surely no great shame in mistakes made in the best of faith. It is surely a thing far more shameful to be unable or unwilling to acknowledge them. (124–25)

Here, Ono appears to "come clean" about his past while, as the reader will see, he actually further suppresses it. In this light Ono's seemingly benign "nostalgic mood" (75) will prove to be anything but unproblematic.

Ono engages in a series of defense mechanisms in order to avoid his past. In particular, he exhibits repression and projection to the extent that he lies to himself, rationalizes past activities, comments upon himself (through others), and selectively filters the past. As Ishiguro himself remarks, "memory is this terribly treacherous terrain" and "the very ambiguities of memory go to feed self-deception."[9] And as Nigel Hunt puts it of the present case, Ono's "memory is always subject to reinterpretation." He "brackets off incidents and their relevance which he does not wish to consider at the moment."[10] It becomes clear, for example, that Ono conveniently forgets certain things and remembers (or misremembers) others in an attempt to allay his feelings of guilt. After recounting some words he uttered while "bravely" standing up for a beleaguered colleague, Ono then admits, "Of course, this is all a matter of many years ago now and I cannot vouch that those were my exact words that morning" (69). At other points Ono claims to remember vividly his actions and words of years earlier, only later to admit, "I can barely recall what had taken place just one week" before (54). Ono is even aware of his own selective remembering—or misremembering—when he observes that the words he recalls uttering in a particular situation "may not have been the precise words" he used, "for I have had cause to recount this particular scene many times before, and it is inevitable that with repeated telling, such accounts begin to take on a life of their own" (72).

Related to Ono's selective memory is his refusal to face his fears directly or openly, a refusal that is mirrored in his grandson's response to a frightening movie that he at one point watches with Ono in a cinema: Ichiro throws a "raincoat over his head" while denying his fear (82). Even more interesting is Ono's proclivity to displace or project his wishes and fears onto others as a means of evading his own feelings. For example, Ono insists that Ichiro wishes to attend the cinema when it is really he who most wishes to attend, and Ono likewise attributes his own disappointment to his grandson when the excursion is temporarily postponed (37–39). Similarly, Ono insists that Ichiro is upset when his mother forbids him to taste sake when it is clearly Ono who is most upset (188–89). And Ono frequently "confuses" the words of others with his own (151, 177), leading the skeptical reader to conclude that this is Ono's preferred means of addressing, however indirectly, his own fears and desires. For example, when Ono celebrates a civic leader, Sugimura, for his grand if failed schemes to improve the city, he celebrates himself ("a man who aspires to rise above the mediocre, to be something more than ordinary, surely deserves admiration, even if in the end he fails . . . on account of his ambitions" [134]). And when Ono rationalizes the failures of an ex-colleague, Matsuda, he rationalizes his own ("He may indeed have looked back over his life and seen certain flaws, but surely he would have recognized also those aspects he could feel proud of" [201]). At the novel's close Ono even seems to speak hopefully about himself when he speaks hopefully about Japan: "Our nation, it seems, whatever mistakes it may have made in the past, has now another chance to make a better go of things" (206).

That Ono suffers from denial is perhaps the most obvious and most telling point. He denies, for example, that the Miyake family has rejected his daughter Noriko because of *his* wartime activities:

My own guess is that there was nothing so remarkable about the matter. True, their withdrawal at the last moment was most unexpected, but why should one suppose from this that there was anything peculiar in it? My feeling is that it was simply a matter of family status. The Miyakes, from what I saw of them, were just the proud, honest sort who would feel uncomfortable at the thought of their son marrying above his station. (18–19)

Ono continually explains away his own role in Noriko's stalled effort to conclude a marriage agreement by blaming the problem on the Miyake family's lack of "prestige" (80) and on bad timing generally: "The war came at a bad time for" Noriko's marital aspirations (84).

Ono also denies that he is now an artistic "has-been" and discredited nationalist; he laughs defensively when Ichiro tells him, "Father says you used to be a famous artist. But you had to finish" because "Japan lost the war" (32). Such denial is most clearly suggested in Ono's repeated refusal to show his grandson his propagandistic wartime artworks, claiming, "They're all tidied away just for the moment" (79). Rather than own up to any past mistakes, Ono merely "tidies" them away, psychologically speaking, and then proceeds to defend himself, insisting that he has "a lot to be proud of" (94): "After all, if your country is at war, you do all you can in support, there's no shame in that" (55).

Ono's denial also extends to the changes taking place in postwar Japan. This is suggested in the countless descriptions of bomb damage and the attempts to rebuild the city, which resonate with Ono's attempt to deny and bury the past and to reconstruct in its place a new reality. In particular, Ono indirectly reveals himself in his descriptions of the changes taking place in the "pleasure district" that he used to frequent and in Mrs. Kawakami, who runs his favorite drinking establishment. While it is clear that Mrs. Kawakami has been "greatly aged by the war years" and that "Business too has become increasingly difficult for her" (23), she and Ono agree that they should "start rebuilding the old days" (76). Although "nothing really remains" of the pleasure district—most bars having "closed up and left" (23) the area, the bombs having left behind only the "skeletal remains" of "charred" and "burnt-out buildings"—Ono nevertheless wonders, "Who is to say the old district will not return again? The likes of Mrs. Kawakami and I, we may tend to make a joke about it, but behind our bantering there is a thread of serious optimism" (77). While the area is now little more than a "wasted expanse," punctuated by "heaps of rubble" and resembling "a graveyard" (27), from which fires arise "like pyres at some abandoned funeral" (28), Ono insists, contradicting the obvious, that Mrs. Kawakami's bar "remains as pleasing as ever" (26). Their crowd is clearly out of favor—"we were as usual alone in the place" (126)—but Ono is loathe to accept this new state of affairs. When he remarks that "one can surely understand" Mrs. Kawakami's "reluctance to accept" that her bar is "gone for ever" (127), Ono describes his own "reluctance to accept" just "how small, shabby and out of place her little bar" has become. Indeed, the little that remains of the old pleasure district amid the new development resembles, like Ono himself, a refugee from a former world, "looking oddly incongruous in its new setting" (205).

Finally, at many points the novel comments on the protagonist's striking denial, as it were, behind his back. This is most evident in the example of the Hirayama boy, a retarded child who gets beaten up for singing "old military songs" and for "chanting regressive slogans" when the war is over (59). In "the years before and during the war" this boy was "a popular figure in the pleasure district with his war songs and mimicking of patriotic speeches" (60). Ono remembers that there were no more than a few songs in his repertoire, and that people would "stop to give him money, or else buy him something to eat, and on those occasions the idiot's face would light up into a smile. No doubt, the Hirayama boy became fixated on those patriotic songs because of the attention and popularity they earned him" (61).

This description serves as an ironic and indirect commentary on Ono's own blindness, naivete, and culpability: like the Hirayama boy, Ono is exposed as lacking in vision, opportunistic, pandering to crowds, and incapable of changing his tune. Like the boy, he is shown to mimic patriotic themes and slogans, and to be incapable of understanding why his message no longer falls on sympathetic ears. Thus, Ono is depicted as closely resembling the boy, even if he sees himself in starkly opposite terms, as the quintessential freethinking, critical artist-citizen: "I do not think I am claiming undue credit for my younger self if I suggest my actions . . . were a manifestation of a quality I came to be much respected for in later years—the ability to think and judge for myself, even if it meant going against the sway of those around me" (69). Ono also comments that men like himself were "all too rare," while the novel suggests just the reverse: that Ono was capable only of succumbing to the political pressures of the moment. Ono takes pride in his always questioning "authority," in never following "the crowd blindly," and in rising "above the sway of things" (73), though the novel, tacitly yet repeatedly, insists otherwise. Indeed, in one of the novel's most ironic moments, Ono challenges a former student, Shintaro, to "face up to the past" by chastising him, "there's no need to lie about yourself" (103–4).

AN ARTIST OF THE FLOATING WORLD

This conflict between teacher and student, superior and inferior, parent and child is a major concern of the novel and lies at the heart of Ono's progress from child to adult, follower to leader, and student to *Sensei* (teacher or master). Ono's development as an artist—from early discouragement by his stern and disapproving father, to apprenticeship, and finally to a leadership position—is figured in terms of this age-old and inevitable conflict. As Ishiguro observes of his novel, "I needed to portray this world where a leader figure held this incredible psychological sway over his subordinates. And for subordinates to break free, they had to display a remarkable amount of determination. . . . I'm pointing to the master-pupil thing recurring over and over again in the world."[11] Indeed, the tensions in this novel between authoritarian art teachers and rebellious students mirror the broader social and political events leading Japan into World War Two.

Ono's first break with an authority figure is with his businessman father who obsesses over his family's finances. Ono's father is displeased that his son wishes "to take up painting as a profession" (43), since he views business and art as antithetical endeavors. He recalls a wandering priest's judgment of long ago that Ono was born "with a flaw in his nature. A weak streak that would give him a tendency towards slothfulness and deceit" (45). If his weak impulses were not checked, the priest predicted, Ono would "grow up to be a good-for-nothing" (45). And Ono's father detects just such a weakness running through his son's character and utters the popular canard against the "decadent" artist: "We've had to combat his laziness, his dislike of useful work, his weak will" (46). "Artists," he adds, "live in squalor and poverty. They inhabit a world which gives them every temptation to become weak-willed and depraved" (46). This scene culminates with Ono's father apparently burning his son's paintings, yet this discouragement, as Ono insists, succeeds only in kindling his artistic ambition (47). As Ono remarks to his mother, "I have no wish to find myself in years to come, sitting where Father is now sitting, telling my own son about accounts and money. . . . What are these meetings I'm so priviledged to attend? The counting of loose change. The fingering of coins, hour after hour" (47–48).

Interestingly, the string of authority figures in this novel who accuse their subordinates of unfilial disloyalty and its corollary, decadence, and who then burn their paintings extends from Ono's father to Ono himself, and includes the *Sensei* Mori-san along the way. Those students of Mori-san's who are found to be painting in a spirit antithetical to the Master "would then abandon the painting, or in some cases, burn it along with the refuse" (140). Mori-san's leading pupils, first Sasaki and then Ono, are deemed "traitors" for "exploring curious avenues." Unless they repudiate their work, they are ostracized by Mori-san's other apprentices and their work is confiscated or burned, presumably by the master himself (142–43, 165, 177).

Ono does subsequently develop self-confidence. For when Mori-san, after accusing Ono of artistic insubordination, commands Ono to bring him all of his other paintings—presumably in order to destroy them—Ono this time refuses; unlike in the earlier episode with his father, Ono here stands up to his superior and refuses to comply with his wishes (178–79). Of course, Ono's refusal to oblige leads to his dismissal from Mori-san's villa. "You will no doubt succeed in finding work illustrating magazines and comic books," Mori-san chides Ono, though "it will end your development as a serious artist" (180). When Mori-san and Ono later trade places in artistic stature, Ono clearly takes a wry satisfaction in surpassing his former teacher (203).

Of course, this reversal of fortune occurs only after Ono has become a *Sensei* who seeks to further Japan's nationalist and imperialist goals, during which time he is unwittingly responsible for having a student's work burned by the "authorities." During this episode Ono is alarmed at the "smell of burning" (181), just as he is alarmed by a government worker's dismissive comment, "Bad paintings make bad smoke" (184). Five years later "the smell of burning still makes" Ono uneasy: "It's not so long ago it meant bombings and fire," he exclaims (200)—not to mention burning paintings.

Ono goes through three artistic stages. His first stage, the "early part" of his career (72), takes place when he is employed by and a student of Master Takeda at the "Takeda firm." At this firm art is a business and quantity is emphasized over quality. Here commercial values rather than aesthetic ones reign supreme, and students are asked to grind out Orientalist, stereotypically Japanese paintings for foreign buyers. Those who paint quickly are rewarded, while those, like the "Tortoise," who are constitutionally slow about their work are chided to paint faster (rather than better). Ironically, having broken away from his father's vulgar materialism, Ono first joins an art business, a "sweatshop"[12] producing local art merely to fill foreign demand. By definition, the stalely conventional work produced by this firm flatters mainstream sentiments; it is unable to shape the future of art or challenge such sentiments. As one of Ono's students later puts it of the Takeda firm, "It sounds more like a firm producing cardboard boxes" (73).

In contrast to his first job at a firm that emphasizes productivity over artistry, profit over self-expression, Ono next spends seven years that he deems "crucial to my career" (137) working for Seiji Moriyama, affectionately known as Mori-san, in an environment in which art and art-making are cut off from quotidian, commercial reality altogether. Rather than engaging the world or satisfying worldly demand, Mori-san's art seeks to "capture the fragile lantern light of the pleasure world" (174), to depict the "intangible and transient" beauty of the "pleasure houses after dark" (150), and to transcend the real world in order to "celebrate" the "floating world" of the novel's title. If Ono's former firm adopts an art-for-profit's-sake mentality, the new firm adopts an art-for-art's-sake one, a formalist agenda; indeed, Mori-san's "decaying villa," in which Ono works and lives "without routine" (87), is the stereotypically bohemian world of the postromantic artist cut off from an inhospitable, materialistic, aesthetically shallow, mainstream society. True to the stereotype, Mori-san's bohemian world involves wanton drinking and the indulgence in sensual pleasures that Ono's father most feared for his son. As Ono at one point puts it of Mori-san's influence: "We lived throughout those years almost entirely in accordance with his values and lifestyle, and this entailed spending much time exploring the city's 'floating world'—the night-time world of pleasure, entertainment and drink which formed the backdrop for all of our paintings" (144–45). Peter Wain astutely observes that Ono's move to the villa "is a different but no less authoritarian environment" than the earlier firm. "There are no targets or deadlines," but his artwork's "content, form and ideological purity must conform to the demands of Mori-san."[13]

Ono's vocational development does not end in Mori-san's villa. Rather, he takes "another step forward" with his artistic career (164) in order to make "work of real importance" that "will be a significant contribution to the people of our nation" (163). This final change of artistic course follows Ono's encounter with Chishu Matsuda of the nationalist and imperialist Okada-Shingen ("New Life") Society. Half seductively, half threateningly, Matsuda insists that Ono's involvement in the society would constitute "an important opportunity to enhance" his reputation (88) and would benefit his "development as an artist" (89). From this new perspective, Ono comes to view Mori-san's attempt to import European currents into his paintings to be "fundamentally unpatriotic" (202–3), and tells his teacher of seven years, "It is my belief that in such troubled times as these, artists must learn to value something more tangible than those pleasurable things that disappear with the morning light. It is not necessary that artists always occupy a decadent and enclosed world" (180).

It is precisely the "real world" in general, and Japanese economic and military aspirations in particular, that Ono hopes to shape and reflect in this third "triumphal" stage of his career. If Ono first apprentices as a hack artist and then as an aesthete, he next finds himself working in the service of Japan's growing nationalist and imperialist aims. Ono comes to serve a "new patriotic spirit" by serving on the "arts committee of the State Department" (63), during which time he reaches the apex of his career and becomes a *Sensei*. His career peaks in 1938 with the conferring of the "Shigeta Foundation Award," which he calls a "major milestone," and with the completion of the "New Japan Campaign" (notice the militaristic ring of this term), which he deems a "great success" (202).

Ono comes to view his two earlier artistic stages as shallow and decadent, respectively, and looks forward to the third by stating that he now seeks "to rise above the undesirable and decadent influences that have swamped us and have done so much to weaken the fibre of our nation" (73). Rejecting the "grotesque" and "frivolous" elements in his midst, Ono now embraces a "new spirit," the "finer, more manly spirit" now emerging in Japan (73–74). Ironically, for one who takes himself to be so freethinking, Ono consorts opportunistically with artists who are "unflinchingly loyal to his Imperial Majesty the Emperor." Also ironically, for one who seeks to distance himself from Morisan's influence, Ono continues to drink heavily. Indeed, Ono and his nationalist cronies come to spend much time in the Migi-Hidari bar because, as he explains it, missing his own irony, "one could get drunk there with pride and dignity" (74). The new direction of Ono's art is underscored by a description of the Migi-Hidari bar, with Kuroda's painting, *The Patriotic Spirit,* hanging on the wall, with "patriotic banners and slogans suspended from the rails of the upper balcony" (74), and with an "enormous illuminated banner . . . bearing the new name of the premises against a background of army boots marching in formation" (64). Tellingly, "Migi-Hidari" is Japanese for "right-left."[14]

Ono also undergoes an evolution *within* this third stage of his career, beginning with a concern for the glaring economic inequalities of his society, and ending with the prostitution of himself and his art to fascist war-aims that are utterly unrelated to the plight of the suffering poor. Ono is suckered into this change by Chishu Matsuda, who comes to have a major impact on Ono's career. Matsuda uses a combination of seduction and coercion to lure Ono to his way of thinking. Dressed "in an elegant white summer jacket" and wearing a "hat slanted down stylishly" (165), Matsuda is portrayed as a charming seducer who flatters in order to capture his prey (you "are someone," he tells Ono, "of immense talent" [173]). Yet he also inspires fear due to his apparent links with brutal, fascist elements. This is suggested when Matsuda tells some intoxicated troublemakers in a bar "to go away," leading Ono to expect trouble: "but something about my companion seemed to unnerve the men, and they left us without comment" (170).

Matsuda also ensnares Ono by showing him the abjectly impoverished Nishizuru district, a fly-infested, squalid, "shanty district" of "open-sewer ditches," whose fate is ignored by politicians, businessmen, and artists alike (166). Places like these, Matsuda tells Ono, "grow everywhere like a bad fungus" (166). In response to the as yet unconverted Ono, who argues that artists should put together an exhibition of their work so as to alleviate the poverty and highlight the plight of the destitute citizens of this district—even if otherwise "An artist's concern is to capture beauty wherever he finds it" (172)—Matsuda counters that Ono's plan is nothing more than naive and childish escapism, a "little good-hearted charity" (172). In such times, Matsuda says, "it is simply not enough for an artist to hide away somewhere, perfecting pictures of courtesans" (173); rather, artists need to be awakened "to the real world," to be removed from their "enclosed little world" (172). "The truth is," Matsuda argues, "Japan is headed for crisis. We are in the hands of greedy businessmen and weak politicians. Such people will see to it poverty grows every day. Unless, that is, we, the emerging generation, take action. . . . The Okada-Shingen exists to help the likes of you open your eyes and produce work of genuine value for these difficult times" (172). Ono's shifting conception of art's proper engagement with worldly concerns is revealed no more clearly than in his evolving portrait of Japan's current crisis and triumphal destiny. The first version of this painting is entitled *Complacency* and the second is called *Eyes to the Horizon.* Both are based on Ono's experience in the Nishizuru district when he sights three boys with "scowls on their faces" who brandish sticks and who appear to be "torturing some animal" (167). In the first painting, *Complacency,* the three boys stand "in front of a squalid shanty hut" dressed in rags; however, here "the scowls on their faces" are not "guilty, defensive scowls of little criminals caught in the act" but instead "manly scowls of samurai warriors ready to fight" (168). Above the head of the three boys the painting fades "into a second image—that of three fat, well-dressed men, sitting in a comfortable bar laughing together. The looks on their faces seem decadent; perhaps they are exchanging jokes about their mistresses or some such matter. These two contrasting images are moulded together within the coastline of the Japanese islands" (168). A caption on the painting reads: "But the young are ready to fight for their dignity" (168). The later *Eyes to the Horizon,* a reworking of the earlier painting after Matsuda's influence on Ono has taken root, also employs two images merging into one another, with the coastline of Japan in the background.

> The upper image was again that of three well-dressed men conferring, but this time they wore nervous expressions, looking to each other for initiative. And these faces . . . resembled those of three prominent politicians. For the lower, more dominant image, the three poverty-stricken boys had become stern-faced soldiers; two of them held bayoneted rifles, flanking an officer who held out his sword, pointing the way forward, west towards Asia. Behind them, there was no longer a backdrop of poverty; simply the military flag of the rising sun. (168–69)

The new caption reads: "No time for cowardly talking. Japan must go forward" (168–69). In the second version of the painting there is no longer any reference to Japan's poverty or economic injustice; rather, the transformed painting emphasizes reactionary, militaristic, imperialist themes. Moreover, rather than eschewing politics, the new version of Ono's painting is unapologetically political, not to mention sloganeering, jingoistic, and dogmatic in the extreme.

That Ono ultimately prostitutes his art to the fascist regime in this third stage of his career becomes painfully obvious. He becomes a dupe of Matsuda, whose ideology he merely parrots. Ono directs the China Crisis poster campaign, joins the "Cultural Committee of the Interior Department," and works as an "official advisor to the Committee of Unpatriotic Activities"

(182). Art and politics now seem intertwined endeavors for Ono. This is made clear when he wins the Shigeta Foundation Award, following which "a chief of police I had never met before" comes to "pay his respects" (202). Moreover, it is hinted that the Okada-Shingen Society, with like-minded people "in politics, in the military" (173), is less an artistic than a political organization that seeks to co-opt Japan's leading artists to support a "restoration" of "his Imperial Majesty the Emperor." As Matsuda maintains,

> Japan is no longer a backward country of peasant farmers. We are now a mighty nation, capable of matching any of the Western nations. In the Asian hemisphere, Japan stands like a giant amidst cripples and dwarfs. . . . It's time for us to forge an empire as powerful and wealthy as those of the British and the French. We must use our strength to expand abroad. The time is now well due for Japan to take her rightful place amongst the world powers. (173–74)

Matsuda's "artistic" society thus seeks the backward-looking goal of empowering the military and his Imperial Majesty the Emperor at the expense of certain "businessmen and their politicians" (173–74), representatives of an open, if economically inegalitarian, society.

The most problematic of Ono's activities during this stage of his career is that he betrays a student, Kuroda, to the police, furthering the goals of the censoring, repressive, fascist regime. Based on information supplied by Ono (182), the authorities remove Kuroda for questioning, torture him in jail as a traitor (113), and burn his paintings, Nazi-style, deeming them "unpatriotic trash" (183) (Ironically, Ono earlier is called a "traitor" for betraying Mori-san's artistic ideals [165]). Admittedly no longer an artistic issue, this action against Kuroda is deemed a "police matter" (183). Now it is Ono who is the oppressive authoritarian, brutalizing an underling, burning the work of a subordinate. Now it is he who plays the role of repressive *Sensei*.

Notably, the novel remains skeptical of all three of Ono's artistic stages: art in the service of purely commercial, aesthetic, or political ends. In this sense, it is less that Ono progresses than that he flounders in his approaches, a fact suggested by Ishiguro's choice for his protagonist's name. "Ono," in English at least, is a palindrome—it reads the same backwards and forwards. Might his circular name suggest a circular fate, that the protagonist is going in circles, as Stevens does literally in his circular journey in *The Remains of the Day*? Might Ono's name suggest his failed past, that he is somehow "chasing his own tail"?

Eventually, Ono comes to fear this very possibility, and works himself around, defensively, to the position that even if he was wrong, at least he was influential: that it is more important to have made one's mark than to have been a right-minded nonentity. In this sense, Ono's entire story—the novel itself—is an attempt to establish his artistic significance, even if he was on the wrong side in the battle for Japan's soul. Like Stevens in *The Remains of the Day,* Ono comes to care more about his professional standing than about the values this standing upholds. In this sense Ono's and Stevens's stories are attempts to negate the fact, as Ishiguro puts it, that "their lives are spoiled because they don't have any extraordinary insight into life. They're not necessarily stupid, they're just ordinary."[15] Ono is obsessed with his prestige, even while pretending not to be. Although insisting that it is not his "instinct to concern" himself with status—"Indeed, I have never at any point in my life been very aware of my own social standing" (19)—Ono experiences "a warm glow of satisfaction" (25) whenever this status is brought to his attention. He is only falsely modest in his claim to being constantly "surprised by the extent" of his influence: "I have never had a keen awareness of my own standing" (21). For example, Ono points out that he won the right to purchase his present house via an "auction of prestige" (9), in which "one's moral conduct and achievement are brought as witnesses rather than the size of one's purse" (10). Openly viewing himself as modest—"I was never one to concern myself with matters of esteem" (64)—he secretly views himself as a man of standing, a "natural leader" (76) whose students always have "an ear open for another piece of knowledge I might impart" (73).

Ono will admit to being wrong as long as he can maintain the illusion of having been influential. As Peter Wain puts it, "as well as his desire to conceal this past of his, there is a pressing vanity that makes him want to be known—to be a celebrity."[16] For example, while Ono is willing to admit that the "sentiments" of *Eyes to the Horizon* are now "perhaps worthy of condemnation" (169), he is not willing to admit that his artistic influence was never truly monumental. Ono is also revealing when he remarks that "I am not too proud to see that I . . . was a man of some influence, who used that influence towards a disastrous end" (192), that "mine was part of an influence that resulted in untold suffering for our own people" (134). For in actuality, the novel broadly hints, he exerted only a marginal influence toward that "disastrous end" and "untold suffering." Perhaps he was both wrong *and* insignificant.

Indeed, the novel suggests that Ono's sense of self-worth is massively inflated, that his reputation during the war years was actually less high than he lets on. This slips out in the present of the novel, when Matsuda tells Ono, "you wanted so badly to make a grand contribution" (199), but then admits, "our contribution was always marginal. No one cares now what the likes of you and me once did" (201). This sentiment is underscored by Ono's daughter Setsuko, who remarks that "Father's work had hardly to do" with Japan's involvement in World War Two. "Father was simply a painter. He must stop believing he has done some great wrong." She even asserts that an old neighbor of Ono's "was unaware that Father was connected with the art world at all" (193), contradicting Ono's claim that his "reputation as a painter" was taken for granted by all (194).

In this sense, *An Artist of the Floating World* concerns the problem of the "parochial perspective"[17]; the novel insists upon its teller's "smallness" even as the teller struggles to appear larger-than-life. As Matsuda later reminds Ono, "we turned out to be ordinary men. Ordinary men with no special gifts of insight" (200).

This lack of insight, in turn, suggests an interpretive bridge between this novel and Ishiguro's third, whose publication followed by only two years. As Ishiguro writes,

> *An Artist of the Floating World* is an exploration of somebody trying to come to terms with the fact that he has some-

how misused his talents unknowingly, simply because he didn't have any extraordinary power of insight into the world he lived in. . . . To a large extent, the reason for Ono's downfall was that he lacked a perspective to see beyond his own environment and to stand outside the [popular] values of his time. . . . The book is largely about the inability of normal human beings to see beyond their immediate surroundings, and because of this, one is at the mercy of what this world immediately around one proclaims itself to be.[18]

This is a phenomenon that Ishiguro would further develop and explore—indeed, take to its logical conclusions and perfect—in the character of Stevens in his next and best-known novel, *The Remains of the Day.*

CHAPTER FOUR

The Remains of the Day

The great butlers are great by virtue of their ability
to inhabit their professional role and inhabit it to
the utmost. . . . They wear their professionalism as
a decent gentleman will wear his suit: he will not
let ruffians or circumstance tear it off him in the
public gaze.

> Stevens,
> in *The Remains of the Day,* 42–43

People are in general not candid over sexual
matters. They do not show their sexuality freely,
but to conceal it they wear a heavy overcoat
woven of a tissue of lies.

> Sigmund Freud,
> *Five Lectures,* 43

In a series of interviews he granted following the publication of *The Remains of the Day* (1989), Kazuo Ishiguro reveals
his own understanding of Mr. Stevens, the novel's first-person
protagonist and aging butler of Darlington Hall, who narrates
his 1956 "expedition" to the English West Country against the
backdrop of an even more significant journey—a journey into
his past life at Darlington Hall during the politically turbulent

1920s and 1930s. In these interviews, Ishiguro emphasizes repeatedly Stevens's "suppression of emotion,"[1] his use of "memory" to "trip" himself up or to "hide" from himself and his past.[2] Stevens, Ishiguro contends,

> ends up saying the sorts of things he does because somewhere deep down he knows which things he has to avoid. . . . Why he says certain things, why he brings up certain topics at certain moments, is not random. It's controlled by the things that he doesn't say. That's what motivates the narrative. He is in this painful condition where at some level he does know what's happening, but he hasn't quite brought it to the front.[3]

Ishiguro here describes the psychic mechanism of repression, a function of the unconscious "that censors, displaces, and condenses dangerous material, driving it from the conscious into the unconscious."[4] Stevens's repression extends to his sexual and political life: to his relationship with his co-worker Miss Kenton, a woman to whom he is deeply attracted, though he never admits it; and to his relationship with his two "fathers," his natural father, also a butler, and his class "father" and master, Lord Darlington, behind whom he hides his "political conscience" and on whom he bestows his loyalty. But while Stevens's repression is difficult to miss, it is easy to overlook the myriad ways in which Stevens *conceals* his striking sexual and political disengagement, by clothing it under a "heavy overcoat woven of a tissue of lies."[5]

THE REMAINS OF THE DAY

This is first hinted at in the novel's prologue, where Stevens initially considers a "five or six day" round-trip expedition to the West coast to visit Miss Kenton (now Mrs. Benn), whom he has not seen in two decades. Here, Stevens muses on the matter of his travelling costumes, the "question of what sorts of costume" would be "appropriate on such a journey, and whether or not" it would be worthwhile investing "in a new set of clothes."[6] Noting that he already possesses "a number of splendid suits, kindly passed on to me over the years by Lord Darlington himself," Stevens nevertheless worries that "many of these suits" may be "too formal for the purposes of the proposed trip, or else rather old fashioned these days" (10). Interestingly, this early, seemingly insignificant, reference to Stevens's "travelling costume" announces one of the novel's chief concerns and controlling metaphors: the literal and figurative ways by which the butler clothes his private self from his own understanding and from the "public gaze." More specifically, it is notable that both literal and figurative forms of clothing function to conceal—yet also, paradoxically, to reveal—Stevens's sexual and political repression to the extent that it is cloaked in the garb of "professional dignity." It is precisely this dignity, after all, that in his view "comes down to not removing one's clothing in public" (210). As Stevens also tellingly insists at one point, "A butler of any quality must be seen to *inhabit* his role, utterly and fully; he cannot be seen casting it aside one moment simply to don it again the next as though it were nothing more than a pantomime costume" (169). Kathleen Wall astutely observes that nothing can "tear the fabric" that Stevens "has erected between his pri-

vate and his professional selves" and that "threatening moments
. . . are shrouded by Stevens in layers of more comfortable
memory."[7]

Stevens's clothes conceal yet also reveal his identity because clothes hide nakedness and conceal true constitutions, yet
they also serve as vehicles of self-expression in that something
about identity is divulged in one's choice of attire. Similarly,
Stevens's narrative "thread," his public presentation of his private life, functions as an attempt to clothe his sexual and political repression, however much it finally reveals about both.
Indeed, his narrative (the novel itself) obscures as much as it
illuminates the true nature of his earlier life at Darlington Hall
and his present voyage west. Although Stevens remains largely
oblivious to it, the novel figures and prefigures this physical trip
as a voyage not only out of the house but out of his mental routine and psychological paralysis in pursuit of amatory and political engagement. The journey, however, fails to accomplish
its purpose, culminating not comically, in his new-found ability
to cast off his "professional suit," but pathetically, in his reaffir-
mation of the necessity of wearing it at all times. The nearly
(spatially and temporally) circular novel closes on a note of "sorry
disappointment" (245), with Stevens's projected return to
Darlington Hall (without Miss Kenton and without a thorough
reassessment of his role in Darlington's political blunders) and
to the "professional" status quo ante.

Ishiguro's use of clothing metaphors is not original. As
Marshall Berman observes, in modern culture "clothes become
an emblem of the old, illusory mode of life; nakedness comes to
signify the newly discovered and experienced truth; and the act

of taking off one's clothes becomes an act of spiritual liberation, of becoming real."[8] What is original about Ishiguro's use of clothing is that Stevens conceals his sexual and political disengagement beneath his "professional suit"; that he hides his avoidance of amatory and social activity beneath the garb of his "professional demeanour" and "emotional restraint" (43). In this sense, it is no surprise that Stevens is incapable of removing what Rousseau calls "the uniform and deceptive veil of politeness" and instead insists upon wearing "mythic draperies heavy enough to stifle" his own self-knowledge.[9] Ishiguro is original in yet another respect: he invokes but then transforms the traditional English novelistic treatment of the relationship between servants and their aristocratic masters. Rather than cutting his master down to size in the eyes of the reader, Stevens instead idealizes Lord Darlington despite his familiarity with his superior's many patent faults. As Frank E. Huggett notes in *Life Below Stairs,* a study of domestic servants in modern England, although some "Victorian servants seem to have had a genuine respect for aristocratic masters," many others were their "constant and inflexible judges. . . . Behind the servants' mask of perfect politeness and consummate gentility, there were dark thoughts and hidden feelings. . . ."[10] In this connection, Salman Rushdie characterizes *Remains* as "a brilliant subversion of the fictional modes from which it at first seems to descend,"[11] while Ihab Hassan maintains that the novel simultaneously "perfects and subverts" its own literary tradition.[12]

Before exploring the ways in which Stevens clothes his repression, it will first be necessary to examine the precise contours of this disengagement, "repression" having become, in John

Kucich's words, "such a buzzword in the post-Freudian world that we rarely reflect on what we mean by it."[13] Freud defines repression as a device protecting "the mental personality," by which "forgotten memories" or "intolerable wishes" are originally "pushed" out of "consciousness." He defines the attendant phenomenon of "resistance" as that force which prevents these "intolerable wishes" from "becoming conscious" and compels them "to remain unconscious."[14] He further argues that the "forgotten material" originates in

> a wishful impulse which was in sharp contrast to the subject's other wishes and which proved incompatible with the ethical and aesthetic standards of his personality. There had been a short conflict, and . . . the idea which had appeared before consciousness as the vehicle of this irreconcilable wish fell a victim to repression, was pushed out of consciousness with all its attached memories, and was forgotten. . . . An acceptance of the incompatible wishful impulse . . . would have produced a high degree of unpleasure; this unpleasure was avoided by means of repression.[15]

Put simply, the essence of repression "lies in turning something away, and keeping it at a distance" from conscious scrutiny.[16]

This "device" for protecting the "ethical and aesthetic standards of personality" illustrates nicely Stevens's ingrained habit of self-deception and self-censorship. Indeed, the butler clearly represses his sexual attraction to Miss Kenton, a woman with whom he works "at close quarters . . . during her maiden years" (47); represses his disappointment upon learning that she is engaged to be married to another (218); represses his "political conscience" through a total identification with his "master," Lord Darlington; and represses his emotional turmoil the evening of his father's death, which he conflates with his successful professional trial-by-fire during that same evening at Lord Darlington's first international political conference—an evening which he now recalls, "for all of its sad associations," with "a large sense of triumph" (110). He also represses his "disappointment" in his entire past, concluding, "Perhaps . . . I should cease looking back so much" and instead "should adopt a more positive outlook and try to make the best of what remains of my day" (244).

Stevens's repression is figured at virtually every turn in the novel. One striking example occurs in 1956 when Stevens is caught denying having known Lord Darlington during the era in which his master was, in effect, aiding, abetting, and appeasing Hitler's war effort. Once caught in this lie, Stevens lies again, rationalizing his betrayal with the claim that although his original explanation was "woefully inadequate," it was not "entirely devoid of truth": "I have chosen to tell white lies . . . as the *simplest means of avoiding unpleasantness.*"[17] But "when one has so much else to think about," the butler adds shortly later, "it is easy not to give such matters a great deal of attention," and so I "put the whole episode out of my mind for some time" (125–26, emphasis added). At other points Stevens is seen *deliberately* refusing to face that which causes him pain, such as when, having run out of fuel, he walks through some muddy fields on the third evening of his journey and dirties the "turn-ups" of his trousers: "I deliberately refrained from shining my lamp on to my shoes and turn-ups for fear of further disappointment" (163). In yet another example, Stevens has the opportunity to comfort Miss Kenton following a death in her family, just as she has sought to comfort him following the death of his father. Kenton loses an aunt who is, "to all intents and purposes, like a mother to her" (176). However, rather than offering Kenton his condolences, as he at first intends, Stevens excuses himself from such activity for fear of intruding "upon her private grief." The belief that she may have been crying provokes "a strange feeling to rise within" Stevens, causing him "to stand there hovering in the corridor" (176–77). And when he later catches up with her, he can only engage her in a "little professional discussion" during which he upbraids her for being "complacent" as regards some new employees under her charge (177–78).

Finally, Ishiguro has Stevens unwittingly and obliquely refer to the unconscious, painful issues that his conscious mind will not let itself address. Comments such as "I had become blind to the obvious" (5) and "I could gain little idea of what was around me" (117) abound, as do various visual metaphors for Stevens's lack of self- and world-engagement. The numerous references to "a mist rolling across" his path (160), "a mist" starting "to set in," a "mist . . . thickening" and "encroaching," a "great expanse of fog" (151–52) describe not only local meteorological conditions but Stevens's self-censoring, self-deceptive psychological orientation. In another example, his melancholy perceptions from the vantage point of old age sum up his entire life of lies and fabrications: "And yet it was not a happy feeling to be up there on a lonely hill, looking over a gate at the lights coming on in a distant village, the daylight all but faded, and the mist growing ever thicker" (162).

More significantly, Stevens's sexual and political repression are figured throughout the novel. That he cannot face his own sexuality is obvious. Not only does the novel virtually open with the new American owner of Darlington Hall, Mr. Farraday, "embarrassing" Stevens by referring to Miss Kenton as his "lady-friend" and by joking about Stevens's sex-life (14–15), but Stevens never addresses Kenton other than by her family name, despite their "close working relationship" (234) for nearly fifteen years. To be sure, Stevens's sexual repression mirrors that of the culture at large. One example of this cultural repression arises when Sir David Cardinal asks Lord Darlington, who then asks Stevens, to explain "the facts of life . . . birds, bees" (82) to his twenty-five-year-old son Reginald Cardinal before he is to be married ("Sir David has been attempting to tell his son the facts of life for the last five years" [82]). Unsurprisingly, Stevens is only too happy to abdicate this responsibility when "professional" obligations prevent him from carrying it out (85, 90).

The most striking examples of sexual repression center around the Stevens-Kenton relationship. Stevens's fear of his own sexuality is associated with his dislike of flowers in his pantry. Indeed, it is associated with his dislike of "distractions" there of any kind, which Kenton persists in supplying. "I am happy to have distractions kept to a minimum" (52), he tells her, and later remembers that Kenton "tried to introduce flowers to my pantry on at least three occasions over the years" (164). Other attractive women are also viewed as distractions Stevens cannot bear. Kenton observes that Stevens does "not like pretty girls on the staff," and then asks, "Might it be that our Mr. Stevens fears distractions? Can it be that our Mr. Stevens is flesh and blood after all and cannot fully trust himself?" (156).

The turning point in their relationship comes in the mid-1930s, when Kenton makes an unmistakable sexual "advance" at Stevens in his pantry. Arriving there with flowers (Stevens believes he remembers), Kenton—who is described as "advancing," "invading," and "pursuing" (166), as if she were trying to break into Stevens's pantry and rip off his clothes—asks to see the book Stevens is reading. Stevens responds by "clutching" the book to his "person," holding the book against his chest, and insisting that she respect his "privacy" (166). Claiming that he is hiding his book because it is "something rather racy" and "shocking," and that she will leave him to the "pleasures" of his reading after he shows her his book, Kenton clearly wishes that Stevens will at last betray a romantic interest. When she finally pries the book from his hands he judges "it best to look away while she did so" (166–67). She discovers, of course, that he is merely reading "a sentimental love story." His claim that he reads these romances strictly "to maintain and develop" his "command of the English language" (167) does not allay but rather heightens the reader's suspicion of his sexual dissociation. Caroline Patey here accuses Stevens of impotence,[18] but it is far more accurate to view this sexual disengagement as repression. This would also explain Stevens's monk-like existence, his choice of quarters, in Kenton's words, "so stark and bereft of colour" (52). In this connection, it is not surprising that Stevens possesses voyeuristic rather than exhibitionistic tendencies. At many points he listens in on others (94, 122, 171, 217), yet he always justifies this spying as due to "professional" considerations.

The parallel example of Stevens's political blindness occurs in the early 1930s. It is when Reginald Cardinal attempts to explain to Stevens that Lord Darlington is being maneuvered by the Nazis "like a pawn" (222), "the single most useful pawn Herr Hitler has had in this country for his propaganda tricks" (224). Naturally, Stevens does not want to acknowledge this, for, if true, it would render Stevens no more than the pawn of a pawn. Insisting that he does not see or notice what is really going on between Lord Darlington and the Germans (223, 224, 225), Stevens represses his own political views, reasoning, "it is not my position to display curiosity about such matters" (222): "I have every trust in his lordship's good judgement" (225). Cardinal's response to Stevens—"you never think to *look* at it for what it is!" (223, emphasis added)—further emphasizes the butler's willed political blindness. In a rare honest moment, Stevens responds to the question, "Have you had much to do with politics yourself," by answering, "Not directly as such" (187).

Yet the clearest—and certainly most compelling—example of Stevens's political repression concerns his total identification not with his lower-class natural father, who suffers both a literal fall (on Darlington's property) and a figurative one (in vocational status), but with his upper-class "cultural" father and master, Lord Darlington. It is clear that Stevens prefers his "gentleman" to his lower-class father, the latter of whom is depicted at one point "pushing a trolley loaded with cleansing utensils, mops, [and] brushes" that "resembled a street hawker's barrow" (78). Although Stevens clearly emulates his natural father's "expression balanced perfectly between dignity and readiness to oblige" (38), his renewed contact with him at Darlington Hall, which begins in 1922, the year of Miss Kenton's arrival, nevertheless precipitates awkwardness and "an atmosphere of mutual embarrassment" (64).

That Stevens substitutes his adopted father for his actual father is made clear during the night that his actual father dies and his master's international conference reaches its climax. At first responding to his dying father's final words to him, "I hope I've been a good father to you," by nervously laughing and repeatedly saying, "I'm so glad you're feeling better now" (97), Stevens then quickly returns downstairs to his conference duties for his master. When his father dies later that evening, Stevens still claims not to have time for him, remarking to Kenton, who offers to close the dead butler's eyes, "Please don't think me unduly improper in not ascending the stairs to see my father in his deceased condition just at the moment. You see, I know my father would have wished me to carry on just now." He then adds, "To do otherwise, I feel, would be to let him down" (196)—but by this point the reader is unsure whether the "him" Stevens wishes not to disappoint is his biological or his class father.

David Gurewich is thus correct but does not go far enough when he states, "it is only through his master that Stevens manages to establish his own worth."[19] Indeed, Stevens's willingness, politically speaking, to be a pawn of a pawn of Hitler betokens not any fascistic political leanings on his part but an "emotional fascism"—an extreme and perverse identification with his father-substitute. Stevens inherits many of Lord Darlington's "splendid suits" over the years (10), just as he assumes his master's political beliefs. Thus, Stevens "becomes" an aristocrat merely by following orders. As he explains to Miss Kenton, "my vocation will not be fulfilled until I have done all I can to see his lordship through the great tasks he has set himself. The day his lordship's work is complete, the day *he* is able to rest on his laurels, content in the knowledge that he has done all anyone could ever reasonably ask of him, only on that day . . . will I be able to call myself . . . a well-contented man" (173). Surprisingly, Stevens's identification with his class father reaches its culminating point after Lord Darlington's death, when Stevens allows others to take him for a gentleman rather than the servant of a gentleman (184–88). When Reginald Cardinal tells Stevens that Darlington has "been like a second father to me" (221), it is even more truly the case for the butler to whom he speaks.

Having observed Stevens's amatory and political disengagement, it remains to discover the means by which the butler attempts to clothe this disengagement—to cover it up or justify it to himself and to his audience—beneath the garb of his "professional suit." At one point Ishiguro comments of *The Remains of the Day,* "It seemed to me appropriate to have somebody who wants to be this perfect butler because that seems to be a powerful metaphor for someone who is trying to actually erase the emotional part of him that may be dangerous and that could really hurt him in his professional area."[20] This remark is interesting but misleading. Rather than viewing Stevens's emotional life as a threat to his professional life, it is far more convincing to view his obsession with "professional dignity" as an *excuse* to remain sexually and politically disengaged; and the obsession with his "professional suit" as an emblem of his desire to keep this repression under wraps. Stevens sublimates his sexual and political aims by directing these to a higher and consequently unobjectionable aim—his professional life. Hence, it is no coincidence that Stevens likens one who cannot "maintain a professional demeanour" to "a man who will, at the slightest provocation, tear off his suit and his shirt and run about screaming" (43). For this reason, Cynthia F. Wong gets things backwards when she writes that "Stevens's motor trip" is a "journey reflecting on his repressed love for Miss Kenton . . . which had resulted from his loyalty to Lord Darlington."[21] Rather, Kathleen Wall is correct to note that "Stevens has attempted to avoid, in his life as well as in his narrative, the voices and needs of the feeling self."[22] In other words, Stevens's professionalism is an excuse to shut "out the messiness of life: sex, marriage, personal interests";[23] it is the "wall" he "labors to construct" against "his regrets,"[24] not the other way around.

Examples of Stevens "clothing" his sexual disengagement beneath his professional costume—his "professional viewpoint" (48), "professional matters" (165), or "professional ambition" (115)—abound. It is clear that he views romantic encounters, with their anarchic, emotionally intimate, informal natures—during which clothing, after all, is often removed—to be a grave threat to the "professional order" of the house. Nothing saddens him more, he admits, than his memory of a housekeeper and an under-butler on his staff deciding "to marry one another and leave the profession": "I have always found such liaisons a serious threat to the order in a house." In particular, Stevens views as a "blight on good professionalism" those "persons—and housekeepers [that is to say, women] are particularly guilty here—

who have no genuine commitment to their profession and who are essentially going from post to post looking for romance" (50–51). However much he wishes to prevent such foolish and wasteful things from happening, he cannot (158). As Kenton asks rhetorically of the unattached Stevens at one point: "Here you are . . . at the top of your profession, every aspect of your domain well under control. I really cannot imagine what more you might wish for in life" (173).

Particularly notable is the way in which Stevens uses his professional identity as a means of masking his obvious attraction to Miss Kenton—obvious to readers even if not to him. When she begins taking days off from Darlington Hall for the first time, for example, Stevens admits, "I found it hard to keep out of my mind the possibility that the purpose of these mysterious outings of Miss Kenton was to meet a suitor. This was indeed a *disturbing notion,* for it was not hard to see that Miss Kenton's departure would constitute *a professional loss* of some magnitude. . . . (171, emphasis added). (Notably, he justifies "prying" into her personal affairs exclusively for "important professional reasons" [234].) Stevens repeatedly and defensively justifies his and Kenton's evening cocoa sessions in the "privacy of Miss Kenton's parlour" as "overwhelmingly professional in tone" (147), as "essentially professional" in character (157), and as exclusively for purposes of "professional communication" (174). But when she enters *his* pantry uninvited—a pantry in which all things must be "ordered—and left ordered—in precisely the way I wish them to be" (165)—revealing her own attraction to him, and forcing him to reveal that he reads romance novels there, he resolves "to set about reestablishing" their "professional rela-

tionship on a more proper basis" (169). And things have not
changed twenty years later when Stevens hides his "growing
excitement" (12) at the prospect of taking the car trip to see her
once again beneath the garb of "professional matters" (5)—beneath the "professional motive" of restaffing Darlington Hall: "I
would expect our interview . . . to be largely professional in
character" (180). At one point Stevens even worries that he has
exaggerated the evidence in her letter that she wishes to return
to "service" at Darlington Hall, calling it "wishful thinking of a
professional kind" (140). As Kathleen Wall concludes, "Stevens
has truncated his life to fit a professional mold"; the word "professional," which arises in inappropriate contexts, "becomes either a disguise for other, more emotional motives or a defense
for his strangely unemotional behavior."[25]

Ishiguro contends that his "butler is a good metaphor for
the relationship of very ordinary, small people to power,"[26] which
announces the other major area Stevens hides within the folds of
his "professional suit": a repressed political conscience. Insisting that a butler's "professional prestige" lies "most significantly
in the moral worth" of his employer (114), and that, as a professional, he serves humanity (117) by serving "the great gentlemen of our times in whose hands civilization" has been entrusted
(116), Stevens contends that "a butler's duty is to provide good
service. It is not to meddle in the great affairs of the nation"
(199). For "it is, in practice, simply not possible to adopt . . . a
critical attitude towards an employer and at the same time provide good service"; a butler "who is forever attempting to for-
mulate his own 'strong opinions' on his employer's affairs is
bound to lack one quality essential in all good professionals:

namely, loyalty" (200). Stevens's sublimation of his political conscience to his professional loyalty is revealed no more clearly than when he remembers that Darlington alone made the decisions "while I simply confined myself, quite properly, to affairs within my own professional realm" (201).

Stevens's political capitulation might have remained insignificant, at least morally speaking, were it not for Lord Darlington's flirtation, in the early 1930s, with anti-Semitism, and his decision, "for the good of this house" (146), to fire two maids from his staff strictly on the grounds that they are Jewish. Naturally, it falls to Stevens to do the firing, forcing him, in David Gurewich's words, to "cross the fine line between the loyalty that is the essence of his professionalism and the blind obedience of 'just following orders.'"[27] And while Stevens claims that "my every instinct opposed the idea of their dismissal," he nevertheless also reasons, "my duty in this instance was quite clear . . . there was nothing to be gained at all in irresponsibly displaying such personal doubts. It was a difficult task, but . . . one that demanded to be carried out with dignity" (148). Raising the matter with Miss Kenton in a "businesslike" way, Stevens counsels her, "we must not allow sentiment to creep into our judgement" (148): "our professional duty is not to our own foibles and sentiments, but to the wishes of our employer" (149).

As for Darlington himself, it is hinted that his "going to bed with Hitler" (politically speaking) is motivated by his homoerotic feelings for the aristocratic German Herr Bremann. Bremann, we read, "first visited Darlington Hall very shortly after the [Great] war while still in his officer's uniform, and it was evident to any observer that he and Lord Darlington had struck up a close friendship. . . . He returned again . . . at fairly regular intervals. . . . It must have been towards the end of 1920 that Lord Darlington made the first of a number of trips to Berlin" (71). Further, when Darlington talks about his German friend, his voice resounds "with intensity" (73). Although this German officer is apparently married, Darlington is never able "to discover the whereabouts of any of Herr Bremann's family" (74). And Stevens describes Darlington's international conferences by reference to the "unbroken lines of gentlemen in evening suits, so outnumbering representatives of the fairer sex" (98), and to the "rather feminine room crammed full with so many stern, dark-jacketed gentlemen, sometimes sitting three or four abreast upon a sofa" (92). Lord Darlington's namesake, moreover, may be the character of the same name in Oscar Wilde's *Lady Windermere's Fan.*

Stevens also uses language and memory itself to clothe a painful reality—and wasted life—from scrutiny. Like Joseph Conrad, who avers that "Words blow away like mist, and like mist they serve only to obscure, to make vague the real shape of one's feelings,"[28] Ishiguro states of the language of his novel, "I'm interested in the way words hide meaning. . . . The language I use tends to be the sort that actually suppresses meaning and tries to hide away meaning."[29] Elsewhere Ishiguro puts this even more baldly: "[*The Remains of the Day*] is written in the language of self-deception."[30]

In this connection, readers have noted that Stevens is "a great manipulator of language,"[31] that he uses "his words and his narrative to convey information to us of which he is unaware."[32] Most significantly, Stevens can talk about himself only when he talks about others; when he talks about himself directly, he is compelled to lie. As with the route of his meandering car trip, his story itself might seem "unnecessarily circuitous" (67), but that is precisely the point: his narrative intentionally impedes his voyage of self-discovery. When Stevens concludes that Lord Darlington's "life and work have turned out today to look, at best, a sad waste" (201), or that Kenton's life has come to be "dominated by a sense of waste" (48), he in fact describes his own "life and work"; when he addresses Kenton's "guilt" at helping to precipitate his father's decline in professional status at Darlington Hall (66–67), he addresses his own; when he speaks of Kenton's "nostalgia" for the Darlington Hall of the old days (49, 180), he accurately reveals his own nostalgia; and when he refers to Kenton's "sadness" and "weariness" (233), he instead registers his own ("you do not seem to have been happy over the years," he tells her [238]). It is clear of whom Stevens really speaks when he remarks that Kenton undoubtedly "is pondering with regret decisions made in the far-off past that have now left her, deep in middle age, so alone and desolate," and that "the thought of returning to Darlington Hall" must therefore be "a great comfort to her" (48). And in those few moments when Stevens actually addresses his own feelings, he fabricates a substitute adjective for a more precise one in order to avoid revealing himself. For example, when he admits to being "tired" (105, 220, 242–3), he really means "sad," "disappointed," or "defeated."

Stevens also uses what he calls the "hindsight colouring" his "memory" (87) as a means of clothing his disengagement. At times he uses the present to escape a failed past; at others he uses the past to escape a failed present.[33] Either way, Stevens's ability always to be somewhere that he is not allows him to live what might be called a vicarious existence during the 1920s, 1930s, and 1940s. It is only in 1956, after all, that he ventures forth from Darlington Hall to see England "at first hand" (28) rather than through "Mrs. Jane Symons's *The Wonder of England*" (11); it is only then that he actively seeks the company of a woman rather than reading "sentimental" love stories from Darlington's romance collection "about ladies and gentlemen who fall in love and express their feelings for each other" (167–68); and it is only at that time that he seeks to engage his "political conscience" rather than blindly follow Darlington's lead. In this way, Stevens's trip to the West Country promises to be an act of self-liberation following a life of self-imprisonment (Kenton tellingly likens Stevens's quarters to "a prison cell," a place "one could well imagine condemned men spending their last hours" [165]; and Farraday rebukes Stevens, "You fellows, you're always locked up in these big houses helping out" [4]). Stevens's present voyage to the West may even be understood as his first (semiconscious) attempt to engage his muted erotic and political dimensions.

Indeed, Stevens's journey is figured as an attempt to break out of the house, out of himself, and out of his physical and psychical routine—to overcome his amatory and political disengagement—in the guise of a "pleasure" trip with business implications, the "professional motive" of restaffing Darlington Hall (13). In this sense, the entire novel, which begins with the sentence, "It seems increasingly likely that I really will undertake the expedition that has been preoccupying my imagination now for some days" (3), concerns Stevens's present attempt to change his life after years of unacknowledged unhappiness, to gain self- and world-knowledge to supplement his "house knowledge" (54). Veiled references to the deeper significance of his proposed trip to the West of England—like Gabriel Conroy's proposed trip to the West of Ireland in James Joyce's "The Dead," replete with sexual and political undertones—are in profusion. In both fictions, a physical voyage is associated with the protagonist's increased understanding of self and world. As Stevens himself seems to detect of his own case, "it is perhaps in the nature of coming away on a trip such as this that one is prompted toward such surprising new perspectives on topics one imagined one had long ago thought through thoroughly" (117).

That the butler's physical departure from Darlington Hall is also figured as a psychological one is suggested early on in *Remains*. Stevens, the reader notes, "motored further and further from the house" until the "surroundings grew strange" around him. "But then eventually the surroundings grew unrecognizable" and he knew that he had "gone beyond all previous boundaries." The psychological dimension of this physical description soon becomes unmistakable: "The feeling swept over me that I had truly left Darlington Hall behind, and I must confess I did feel a *slight sense of alarm* . . ." (23–24, emphasis added). Of course, Stevens would never have ventured forth from Darlington Hall during the time when Darlington himself lorded over the house; it is the new American owner, Farraday, who urges Stevens to "get out of the house for a few days" (4). That Stevens initially finds this proposal extravagant is underscored by the fact that he worries that such a journey may keep him away from

Darlington Hall "for as much as five or six days" (3). Perhaps for this reason Ihab Hassan calls the novel a "mental journey, a grudging access to Stevens' past."[34]

Despite Stevens's implicit desire to throw off the yoke of his repression, however, he resists the temptation. Put in the novel's own metaphor, the butler is involved in a struggle between the side of him that wishes to cast off his clothing and the side that wishes to keep it securely wrapped about him. Evidence of this internal conflict is rife. Not only does Stevens, at one point in his voyage, refrain from exploring some beautiful English countryside for fear of "sustaining damage" to his "travelling suit" (121), but initially he responds negatively to Farraday's proposal that he take the trip to see his own country, countering, "It has been my privilege to see the best of England over the years" right within the walls of Darlington Hall itself (4). He adds that he remains reluctant "to change too much of the old ways" (7) and that "strange beds have rarely agreed" with him (47).

Stevens, of course, does not succeed in overcoming his repression. On the political front, Stevens does not gain true insight about his own political disengagement; there is no change in what David Gurewich calls "Stevens's lack of awareness of the world outside his master's estate."[35] Specifically, his encounter with the middle-class Harry Smith, who represents democratic "political conscience" (209), who has strong political opinions, and who therefore stands in stark opposition to the politically disengaged Stevens, makes no impact on the butler whatsoever. While the "common" Smith remarks that "it's one

of the privileges of being born English that no matter who you
are, no matter if you're rich or poor, you're born free and you're
born so that you can express your opinion freely, and vote in
your member of Parliament or vote him out" (186), that
"England's a democracy, and . . . it's up to us to exercise our
rights, everyone of us" (189), Stevens stubbornly adheres to his
earlier aristocratic, oligarchic perspective: "There is, after all, a
real limit to how much ordinary people can learn and know, and
to demand that each and every one of them contribute 'strong
opinions' to the great debates of the nation cannot, surely, be
wise" (194). Smith also contends that protecting democracy is
"what we fought Hitler for": If "Hitler had had things his way,
we'd just be slaves now" (186). Yet this comment is more telling of Stevens's situation than either realizes: Stevens indirectly
worked for Hitler and directly worked to maintain his own status as a "slave," at least intellectually speaking, of Lord
Darlington.

That Stevens fails to overcome his sexual repression is
equally clear. This fact is mirrored in the "ferocious downpour"
of rain, the "ominous stormclouds," the "gloomy" light, and the
subsequent "drizzle" (232, 238) that surround the present meeting between Stevens and Kenton. It is appropriate that rain falls
when they meet; just as between Gabriel and Gretta in Joyce's
"The Dead," precipitation foreshadows a downpour of tears (hers
at 240; his at 243) that betokens a love affair that pales in com-
parison with what it might have been. Indeed, the entire novel
prepares its readers for the Stevens-Kenton encounter which,
however superficially "pleasant" for him, is a brief, uneventful

disappointment: rather than returning to service at Darlington Hall, Kenton vows instead to return to her husband from whom she has been separated.

Ironically, given the expectations that the novel raises in its readers, the gap between Stevens's private belief and public expression—his inner feeling and outer demeanor—is never so wide as in this final chapter. There, Stevens consistently calls his former co-worker "Mrs. Benn" to her face but "Miss Kenton" to himself; and he literally smiles at her even though his "heart [is] breaking" (239). This duplicity enables the forlorn Stevens to convince himself that, despite a clearly failed excursion and life, "there is plenty of daylight left"—that "the evening" may well be "the best part of the day" (240). Despite breaking down when speaking with a retired butler whom he encounters two days after his meeting with Kenton, lamenting that he "gave it all to Lord Darlington" who "at least" had "the privilege of being able to say at the end of his life that he made his own mistakes" (243), Stevens insists that his tears are due only to the fatigue that follows travelling: "I'm so sorry, this is so unseemly. I suspect I'm over-tired. I've been travelling rather a lot, you see" (244). He adds, "Surely it is enough that the likes of you and I at least *try* to make our small contribution count for something true and worthy. And if some of us are prepared to sacrifice much in life in order to pursue such aspirations, surely that is in itself, whatever the outcome, cause for pride and contentment" (244). Stevens's concluding thoughts are surprising—after all, he has voyaged such a long way to go nowhere at all (Stevens's car voyage forms a giant circle across South and West England, suggesting in geographical terms that he is merely going around in circles or "spinning his wheels" in personal or psychological terms)—until they are construed within the context of his failure to overcome his disengagement, to cast off the "professional suit" that is a metaphor for his repression.

Stevens does make one new resolution that appears to be a viable way for him to gain necessary emotional intimacy with others: he will learn to "banter," to engage in conversations of "a light-hearted, humorous sort" (13). In "bantering," Stevens now contends, "lies the key to human warmth" (245). But while Stevens is not being ironic here, Ishiguro undoubtedly is. For Stevens's new resolution clearly can provide no new solution. Like Stevens's first-person narrative style itself, which, as Ishiguro writes, is as much a "form of cowardice" as dignity, "a way of actually hiding from what is perhaps the scariest arena in life, which is the emotional arena,"[36] bantering actually precludes rather than enables the "human warmth" that Stevens now hints would be desirable. This is suggested by a standard ancillary definition of bantering—"to delude or trick, especially by way of jest." For this secondary definition, bantering functions less to promote intimacy than to maintain distance. In this sense *The Remains of the Day* ends neither comically nor tragically (despite the deathly resonances of the novel's title)[37] but on a pathetic and ironic note, as "old habits" of Stevens's "mind reassert themselves in a new guise."[38]

The Remains of the Day is one of the most profound novelistic representations of repression masquerading as professionalism, yet it is also aimed at an entire nation's mythical sense of itself. Indeed, the novel associates Stevens's deceptive self-conception with that of England's at large. Stevens equates the significance of events in Darlington Hall with those in England generally, confuses "house knowledge" with world-knowledge, and moves freely between the subject of what makes a "great butler" great and what makes "Great Britain" great, arguing that both exhibit "calmness" and a "sense of restraint" (28–29). And Stevens clearly equates a decline in the status of Darlington Hall[39] with the postwar Americanization of England[40] and with what David Gurewich calls "the disintegration of the good old world where Stevens and his ideals held value."[41] (It is probably no coincidence that the present of the novel is set in July of 1956, the time of the Suez crisis—"a turning point for the British Empire,"[42] which decisively marked the end of England's claim to world military supremacy.) Yet if Stevens exhibits a nostalgia for this "good old world" of "grand old English houses," *The Remains of the Day* does not, just as *An Artist of the Floating World* subtly if devastatingly throws into ironic relief Ono's nostalgia for the ancien régime in Japan. *Remains* exhibits only a mock nostalgia, one that throws into question the "good old world" as much as it does the grandeur of Stevens's "professional dignity." As Ishiguro himself maintains,

> The kind of England that I create in *The Remains of the Day* is not an England that I believe ever existed. . . . What I'm trying to do there . . . is to actually rework a particular myth about a certain kind of mythical England . . . , an England with sleepy, beautiful villages with very polite people and butlers . . . taking tea on the lawn. . . . The mythical landscape of this sort of England, to a large degree, is harmless nostalgia for a time that didn't exist. The

other side of this, however, is that it is used as a political tool. . . . It's used as a way of bashing anybody who tries to spoil this "Garden of Eden."[43]

Ishiguro undermines this particular ideal of England by showing how the soil in this "Garden of Eden" could nourish the seeds of a destructive fascism, and how the protagonist's professionalism—which nurtures those same seeds—could mask a self-destructive, paralyzing disengagement. *The Remains of the Day* would not prove to be the author's final statement on professionalism and repression, however, anymore than *An Artist of the Floating World* would be his final statement on artistry or *A Pale View of Hills* on dysfunctional family dynamics. All of these concerns would reappear with a vengeance in Ishiguro's fourth, lengthiest, most openly experimental novel, *The Unconsoled.*

CHAPTER FIVE

The Unconsoled

The world seems full of people claiming to be
geniuses of one sort or another, who are in fact
remarkable only for a colossal inability to organise
their lives.

Ryder,
in *The Unconsoled,* 146

At many points in Kazuo Ishiguro's *The Unconsoled* the
protagonist, Ryder, registers "a curious, dreamy sense of unreality" coming over him.[1] This unreality is an experience with which
the reader early on in the text becomes equally familiar, and
which sharply sets off the author's fourth novel from his previous three. *The Unconsoled* represents a clear change of tone,
direction, and scope for Ishiguro. Not only is his fourth work the
length of his first three novels combined, but it also offers in its
expanded form a new dimension—at once absurdist and uncanny,
dreamlike and tragicomic—that recalls the work of Kafka and
Beckett and that both parodies and stretches the conventions of
prose fiction. The novel likewise exhibits some of the openly
experimental play with time, space, and perception associated
with literary modernism and metafiction. As Stanley Kauffmann
astutely sums up this work's break with the author's earlier works,
in *The Unconsoled* Ishiguro moves

THE UNCONSOLED

from the taciturn beauty of the earlier books to a larger scope, a much more explicitly intricate structure—a move from Japan and Britain to the heart of Middle Europe. Previously, he dealt with the psychological and spiritual aftermath of World War II in Japan, then with English confusions and self-betrayals in that war. Now he moves to the continent, to the involuted psyche and spirit that was the root of much of that war, that bred most of our culture and also of our horror.[2]

For Richard Rorty, by contrast, this break is largely stylistic in nature: Ishiguro shifts from a Jamesian to a Kafkaesque prose style.[3]

Reviewers who stress *The Unconsoled*'s break with its author's earlier fiction, however, often overlook those characteristics that the novel shares with the earlier works, characteristics that will help shed light on Ishiguro's most complex and difficult work to date. In the fourth novel, for example, we encounter once again a first-person protagonist who paradoxically conceals yet at the same time reveals elements of his past life and present reality. Moreover, as Amit Chaudhuri writes, "In *The Unconsoled,* the themes of guilt and fear of humiliation persist, as do the means of negotiating them: excessive, insincere flattery, elisions, voluntary and involuntary amnesia."[4] Like *An Artist of the Floating World, The Unconsoled* concerns the problematic position of the artist in society, even though Ryder is a distinguished pianist rather than a painter, like Ono, of uncertain stature. Like *The Remains of the Day, The Unconsoled* interrogates "professionalism" as well as the myriad shortcomings that often hide behind professionalism—though the "workaholic" in the fourth novel is "the finest pianist in the world" (507) rather than a butler. Like *A Pale View of Hills, The Unconsoled* explores child abuse and the various emotional aftershocks that commonly follow it into adulthood; indeed, in both mood and theme, Ishiguro's fourth novel is perhaps closest to his first. Paul Bailey's criticism of *Pale View,* for example, is yet more germane to *The Unconsoled:* "At certain points I could have done with something as crude as a fact."[5] Indeed, concrete facts are even more conspicuously absent, even more difficult to discern, in Ishiguro's latest, funniest, and most disturbing novel. As Pico Iyer puts it, "In many ways, *The Unconsoled* marks a return to the Ishiguro we knew before *The Remains of the Day,* a writer whose first two novels were haunting, and entirely enigmatic."[6]

The Unconsoled centers on the English pianist Ryder—as with Stevens, the reader never learns the protagonist's first name—during his two-and-one-half day visit to an unidentified (but apparently Middle European) city to give a recital and to address this city's never fully articulated cultural "crisis." The four-part novel follows Ryder's Tuesday afternoon through Friday morning visit in and around town. More obliquely, it also explores the protagonist's distant and intermediate past. The dramatic climax of the novel is the much-anticipated Thursday night "event," during which Ryder is to give his recital and otherwise help inaugurate the town's fresh artistic course. On his performance and on the event generally, the reader is told, will "hinge" (375) the town's entire future identity ("Gravely important issues lie behind tonight's occasion. . . . Issues relating to our future, to the very identity of our community" [482]). Ryder never actually gives the recital or addresses the "Citizens' Mutual Support Group" before leaving for his next engagement in Helsinki; these are only two of the novel's more significant expectations—for the protagonist and reader alike—to be slowly raised and then abruptly dropped.

It would be tempting to dismiss the self-important Ryder as an egomaniac were it not for the numerous comments attesting to his artistic prowess showered on him by virtually all of the townspeople he encounters. For example, he is called "not only the world's finest living pianist, but perhaps the very greatest of the century" (11), a "brilliant musician, one of the most gifted presently at work anywhere in the world" (187), and an "internationally recognized genius" (301). It is perhaps because of rather than despite this acclaim that Ryder's personal life, as the reader glimpses it, is in shambles. As Merle Rubin observes, "Ryder is portrayed as having been too busy with his career to spend enough time with his family and as someone who allows his daily activities, sometimes his very thoughts, to be shaped by the demands of his so-called public."[7] Strangely, the precise nature of his personal life is as difficult for Ryder as it is for his readers to discern. But glimpse it, at least, his readers do: via Ryder's vague and elliptical memories and via the novel's other characters, each of whom is revealed to have a pathologically self-destructive personal life that significantly mirrors Ryder's own. As Rubin puts it, "Not only Ryder, but everyone else in town seems caught in a trap of his or her own making."[8]

Virtually all of the people Ryder encounters during his brief stay in town want something from him—inappropriate things that, despite the pianist's best intentions, he cannot provide—and employ flattery of grotesque proportions to attain it. Moreover, they inexplicably confess their innermost fears and desires to Ryder, a man who is, to all appearances, a complete "outsider" to their lives, a visitor merely passing through the unnamed town. The most uncanny and unnerving of the novel's suggestions, however, is that Ryder may in fact be an *insider* to their unconsoled and unconsolable realities, and that, like Stevens, he must repress the stark knowledge of his own past traumas and "tangled knots of emotion" (357) and hide behind the demands of his professionalism.

Of the minor characters, old friends Ryder has not seen in decades (why do they live in this city anyway? might Ryder come from this place after all?) make small requests of him. Mr. Christoff, the deposed conductor of the town's symphony orchestra, asks Ryder to "modify" his "present stance" (187) (readers never learn the precise nature of that stance) and help him restore his earlier artistic prestige; and sycophantic journalists exaggeratedly (and amusingly) badger Ryder for interviews and photo sessions that only end up getting him in trouble with the locals he most wishes to impress and appease.

Of the major characters, three clusters of three people each are most germane to an understanding of Ryder's situation. These characters, while "real," are mainly to be understood as extensions, versions, or variations of Ryder himself—individuals, like Sachiko for Etsuko in *A Pale View of Hills,* through whom he projects his own story. While these characters should not be regarded as mere fabrications of the protagonist's, then, they should be understood as conduits for Ryder to remember and forget, judge and censor his own past. First is a triangle comprising the Polish Leo Brodsky, once an illustrious conductor but more recently an embarrassing eccentric, a depraved lunatic, the "town drunk" (522), whom many wish to resuscitate as a replacement for Christoff; Miss Collins, the wife from whom Brodsky has been estranged for two decades; and Bruno, Brodsky's beloved, recently deceased dog (and child substitute). Brodsky wants Ryder both to help him win back Miss Collins and to play the piano to accompany the burial of his beloved dog ("I want to say goodbye" to Bruno properly; "I wanted the best music" [330]).

Second is a triangle comprising Hoffman, the manager of the hotel in which Ryder is staying during his visit and the chief mover behind Brodsky's restoration as conductor; Christine, Hoffman's wife; and Stephan, their son. Hoffman, the most mysterious of the novel's characters, wants Ryder to help him get Brodsky into shape for the all-important Thursday concert; Christine, according to Hoffman, wants Ryder to inspect her voluminous albums of press cuttings outlining his distinguished international career; and Stephan wants Ryder to listen to and evaluate a sample of his piano playing in advance of Thursday night's program.

Third is the triangle comprising Gustav, the hotel porter who helps Ryder with his bags upon his arrival at the hotel; Sophie, Gustav's daughter, with whom the porter has not been on speaking terms for years, and with whom Ryder might have had a significant relationship in the past; and Boris, Gustav's young grandson (and Sophie's son), who is also possibly Ryder's son (the reader never knows for certain). Gustav wants Ryder to speak with Sophie and help her "recover her sense of perspective" ("she has this tendency to let things overwhelm her" [28]), and he later asks Ryder to say "a few words" on behalf of the town's hotel porters at the Thursday night gathering, "to try and change the attitude in this town towards" members of his profession (296); Sophie wants Ryder to help her find a new residence in which they can all live together; and Boris wants Ryder to accompany him to the "old apartment" (where they all may once have lived together) to recover a miniature toy soccer player left behind.

What further unites these characters is that all of them are obsessed with their various fears and desires: Boris with his toy; Sophie with her father's winter coat and the hunt for a home; Gustav with his daughter and his "professionalism"; Stephan with his parents; Ryder with his parents and career; Brodsky with Miss Collins and his dog; and Hoffman with his job and wife. Moreover, they are perfectionists who fail in whatever they set out to accomplish: Sophie and Boris do not recover Ryder; Gustav dies never fully making amends with Sophie, with whom he has not been on speaking terms for the most absurdly trivial of reasons; Stephan disappoints his parents at the concert; Hoffman cannot restore Brodsky or impress his wife; and Brodsky does not recover Miss Collins. Finally, Ryder disappoints each of them in some significant way: he never signs the albums, speaks on behalf of Gustav, makes things up with Sophie and Boris, restores Brodsky, or even performs Thursday night. Precisely why he declares himself "well satisfied with what I had achieved in the short time since my arrival" (158) remains a mystery. More appropriate is one citizen's worry that Ryder may be in town merely on a "fool's errand" (108), merely as an "unwitting pawn in other people's incomprehensible dramas.'"[9] Perhaps there is more relevance to Ryder's discovery at one point that he is walking "in circles" (212) than even he knows.

No discussion of *The Unconsoled* would be complete without treating what Vince Passaro calls the novel's "severe dreamlike quality"[10]—its absurd, uncanny, paranoia-inducing, Kafkaesque dimensions. The novel is particularly Kafkaesque in its paradoxically distorted yet veristic representations. As Erich Heller explains, "Kafka's style—simple, lucid, and 'real' in the sense of never leaving any doubt concerning the reality of that which is narrated, described, or mediated—does yet narrate, describe or mediate the shockingly unbelievable."[11] Heller's description of Kafka's style also explains *The Unconsoled*'s unrelenting dreamlike absurdity. Examples of this absurdity abound: the "ticket inspector" on a tram Ryder gets on happens to be a hostile childhood friend (170–71); a cafe Ryder chances by is filled with diners enjoying "steaming bowls of what looked to be mashed potato," which they eat "hungrily with long wooden spoons" (192); he witnesses porters frenetically engaged in a "Porter's Dance" atop tables in another cafe (396); he observes patrons in a cinema casually playing cards and carrying on in small groups (103); his hotel room turns out to be "the very room that served" as his "bedroom during" one phase of his childhood (16); and a funeral-in-progress he chances upon is interrupted so that mourners can greet Ryder and offer him refreshments (366–70). Absurdly, Ryder processes each of these uncanny events as if they were likely, ordinary, to be expected. One excerpt will suffice to convey the novel's pervasive dreamlike flavor. It is when Ryder, in the concert hall in which he is to perform, discovers "a cupboard" through which patrons can see "down onto the auditorium from a vast height."

> The entire back of the cupboard was missing and, were I reckless enough, I saw that I could, by leaning out and stretching a little, touch the concert hall ceiling. The view certainly was commanding, but the whole arrangement struck me as idiotically hazardous. The cupboard, if anything, actually leaned forward, encouraging a careless spectator to totter towards the edge. Meanwhile only a thin cord tied at waist height had been provided to resist a plunge down into the audience. I could not see any obvious reason for the cupboard. . . . (476–77)

Yet Ryder never really questions the point of this cupboard; like "a dreamer, he accepts absolutely the arbitrary and silent logic of his dream."[12]

The novel is also dreamlike in being uncanny, a quality about which Freud has much to say. In his famous essay on the uncanny Freud associates uncanniness with a state of spatial disorientation: the uncanny is always "something one does not know one's way about in."[13] Uncanny works typically "keep us in the dark for a long time about the precise nature" of the worlds they depict.[14] In this connection, it is no surprise that Ryder lacks a firm grasp of his mission in the town and of his past. Many of Ryder's acts prove to be controversial (such as his posing for pictures in front of the Sattler monument), though he never learns why, just as, contrarily, a speech he never actually delivers is received as a "marvellously witty address!" (155): "Everyone's been talking about it, all over the city. It really was such a charming speech" (160). Even his much discussed "delayed arrival" (18), it is hinted, is his fault, though he has no knowledge of what delayed him or of how or why he may be to blame.

This uncanny experience of disorientation only mounts as *The Unconsoled* unfolds. Stanley Kauffmann observes *The Unconsoled*'s "vivid but intentionally unreliable continuum of place";[15] and this is also true of its depiction of time. For example, Ryder drives out of the city into the countryside for what appears to be hours, only to make the return trip in minutes; different buildings and locations absurdly conflate into one another, following which Ryder accepts the altered spacial reality as logical; Ryder sleeps for what appears to be hours when it is only minutes, and vice versa; and Ryder's early hotel elevator ride with Gustav seems to take half an hour but only lasts moments (5–11). No concrete grasp of time is available in the world of this novel; there are no clocks or watches to be found anywhere, and Ryder can only judge the time by gauging the degree of light or darkness outside. Moreover, even perspective takes on uncanny proportions: Ryder, though a first person narrator, nevertheless can see and overhear conversations going on in places where he is not present (56–57); and he can reveal what other characters are pondering or remembering, just by looking at them ("I caught sight of his profile . . . and realised he was turning over in his mind a particular incident from several years ago" [65–66]).

Freud links the uncanny with the "frightening," with "what arouses dread and horror."[16] More specifically, he links it with a "class of the frightening *which leads back to what is known of old and long familiar.*"[17] This describes perfectly Ryder's (and the reader's) experience in *The Unconsoled:* a feeling of dread arising out of a paradoxical conjunction of strangeness and familiarity. One example of this "familiarity-in-strangeness" will suffice: "When I studied them in turn," Ryder reports, "each door looked vaguely familiar, but I found I did not feel confident about any of them" (278). Freud also relates the uncanny to "the sense of helplessness experienced in some dream states,"[18] on the one hand, and with the "most remarkable coincidences of wish and fulfillment,"[19] on the other—opposed states that are alternately experienced by Ryder. Evidence pointing to the wish fulfillment side of this equation is abundant: public buses seem to wait for Ryder in order to take him precisely where he wishes to go ("this tram will get you more or less anywhere you like in the city" [533]); food is served on the public buses and trams on which he rides (206, 533); long-lost relatives appear out of nowhere (222); and events frequently happen just as Ryder expects them to, as in the logic of a dream: "to my horror, the very thing I had most feared occurred" (278). Examples of the opposed state—of performance anxiety and impediments to wish fulfillment—are also plentiful: Ryder experiences a traffic-jam in the middle of the night, precisely when he is most in a hurry (119); Hoffman keeps changing Ryder's hotel room, never allowing him to get comfortable in any one of them; Ryder, when verbally attacked, discovers that he is unable to defend himself and can only helplessly "grunt" and "panic" (239); the concert hall audience and seats vanish just when Ryder most wishes to perform (519); Ryder feels "pressure" (38) from the people of the city—"much was expected of me here" (26)—yet is not clear on how to satisfy them; and Ryder does not have enough time to prepare or even dress for a speech he is expected to give (134–35), with disastrous results: I "was about to embark on my talk when I suddenly became aware that my dressing gown was hanging open, displaying the entire naked front of my body" (143). Two other absurd examples of impediments to the fulfillment of Ryder's wishes are worth noting. In one instance, Ryder is frustrated in his attempt to secure the proper time and place to practice for his upcoming recital, and, when he finally secures these, realizes that he has been given an imperfectly renovated bathroom in which to rehearse (340). In the other, when Ryder is in a great hurry to reach the concert hall and is only a block away, he encounters "a brick wall running across my path—in fact, across the entire breadth of the street," completely sealing off his destination. Ryder himself deems the wall a preposterous obstacle and an "absurd setback" (387–88); it is no wonder that he registers a "sense of futility" (436) and a "powerful mixture of frustration, panic and anger" (436) at so many points during his short visit to the city.

Samuel Beckett's influence also can be felt in this novel, particularly in its more absurdly comic, ridiculously slapstick moments. As Vince Passaro observes, *The Unconsoled* moves "quickly between anxiety and comedy—in the manner" of "Beckett and other high modernists."[20] Examples of this comic absurdity abound: blandly, conventionally posed photographs of Ryder taken to accompany a newspaper interview turn out utterly unlike Ryder's original poses. Instead, "my features bore an expression of unbridled ferocity. My fist was raised to the wind, and I appeared to be in the midst of producing some warrior-like roar. I could not for the life of me understand how such a pose had come about" (267). In another example, Brodsky's kitchen turns out to be "an outhouse connected to the main farmhouse that Mr. Brodsky has been very skilfully converting" (433). In yet another, no one seems to notice that Brodsky, at Thursday night's concert, is missing a leg, presumably due to a car accident moments earlier, or that the leg he has lost is an artificial one (464). Indeed, at the concert Brodsky is forced to support his weight with a crutch that, on closer inspection, turns out to be "an ironing board" held "vertically and folded, under his armpit" (455). As far as Ryder can discern, "the audience seemed not to notice the missing leg at all," but then Brodsky took a few more steps across the stage and "something on the ironing board gave way. It began to unfold itself under him just as he was placing his weight on it, and Brodsky and the board went down in a heap. . . . At times he appeared to be attempting to stand up, at others he seemed more intent on extricating some part of his clothing from the mechanisms of the ironing board" (489–90). Such a scene would not be out of place in *Waiting for Godot*.

The most significant piece of information that Ryder (and his readers) cannot quite determine, however, is whether or not Sophie and Boris are Ryder's wife and son. Moreover, it remains unclear whether or not Ryder is an "outsider" to the city and its inhabitants, as he keeps insisting, or an insider. While he is patently new to town, the hotel manager, Hoffman, gestures to Ryder in an "unduly familiar" way (20). And while Ryder appears not to know Sophie and Boris when he initially meets them, we begin to get the impression that he may know the two intimately after all. Ryder first describes Sophie as if he has never seen her before ("she was somewhat more attractive than I had expected" [32]); yet when he introduces himself to her she tells Boris that "Mr. Ryder" is "a special friend," and adds shortly later, "a very special friend" (32–33). Ryder then begins to recall a prior acquaintanceship between them: "For the fact was, as we had been sitting together, Sophie's face had come to seem steadily more familiar to me," so that after "a while, I found a faint recollection returning to me of listening to this same voice— or rather a harder, angrier version of it—on the end of a telephone in the not-so-distant past" (34–35). Shortly later, Sophie informs Ryder that Boris wants "to show you the progress he's made" on the swings at the park (36), suggesting an earlier relation of some intimacy. Soon Ryder is promising Boris a trip back to their "old apartment" to "fetch Number Nine" (43), his toy soccer player. When they finally arrive there, the "old apartment" at first arouses no memories in Ryder at all, but then grows "steadily more familiar," while objects inside bring to Ryder "poignant nudge[s] of recognition" (213–14). Ryder and others he encounters soon refer to Boris as his "boy" or his "little boy" (45, 50, 54, 155, 203), just as they refer to Ryder as Boris's "Papa" (286) or "father" (407). A passing stranger even remarks of Ryder and Boris, "It's good to see a father and son getting on so well" (207). At other points, however, a note of uncertainty is reintroduced, such as when Sophie chastises Ryder: Boris is "not your own. Whatever you say, it makes a difference. You'll never feel towards him like a real father" (95).

Unsurprisingly, in this connection, Ryder experiences repression, resistance, and denial—and the return of painful memories long repressed—at many points in *The Unconsoled*. For

example, we read of the return of "certain fragments" (94) of
Ryder's memory ("my memory would unlock and I would finally remember" [24]), of the "opening up of old wounds" (60),
of keeping painful memories "shut out" of his "mind" (360),
and of putting certain "thoughts away for ever" (364). At one
point Ryder even remembers how a childhood friend would comfort him by "allowing me quickly to forget whatever scene I had
just left behind" (239).

The reader is given few specifics, but it becomes apparent
that Ryder has suffered "some hurt in childhood"[21] and that he
has developed various coping skills, among them repression, to
help him to "forget," yet also to capitalize on, his earlier trau-
matic experiences. As early as the first chapter the reader encounters a striking, if indirect, reference to Ryder's developing
repression. As a child of six or seven in England he remembers
playing on the floor of his bedroom one afternoon, when

> a furious row had broken out downstairs. The ferocity of
> the voices had been such that . . . I had realized this to be
> no ordinary row. But I had told myself it was nothing and,
> resting my cheek back down on the green mat, had contin-
> ued with my battle plans. Near the centre of that green
> mat had been a torn patch that had always been a source of
> much irritation to me. But that afternoon, as the voices
> raged on downstairs, it had occurred to me for the first
> time that this tear could be used as a sort of bush terrain
> for my soldiers to cross. This discovery—that the blemish
> that had always threatened to undermine my imaginary
> world could in fact be incorporated into it—had been one

of some excitement for me, and that 'bush' was to become a key factor in many of the battles I subsequently orchestrated. (16–17)

Clearly, Ryder deals with his troubling "family matters" (86)—with his parents' absorption in their frequent fights and with their attendant neglect of him—via a strategy of denial, fantasy, sublimation, and, later, music-making. In other words, as Kathleen Wall puts it of Stevens in the earlier novel, Ryder shrouds "threatening moments" in "layers of more comfortable memory."[22]

The few glimpses that readers do have of Ryder's childhood—and of his developing defense mechanisms—are extremely troubling. During his present visit, Ryder encounters an abandoned, rusty, dilapidated, fungus-covered vehicle, which he recognizes as "the remains of the old family car" that his father drove during his childhood:

Seeing it again in this sad state brought back to me its final days with us, when it had become so old I was acutely embarrassed my parents should continue to go about in it. Towards the end, I recalled, I had started to invent elaborate ploys to avoid taking journeys in it, so much did I dread being spotted by a schoolfriend or a teacher. But that had only been at the end. For many years I had clung to the belief that our car—despite its being quite inexpensive—was somehow superior to almost any other on the road and that this was the reason my father chose not to replace it. (261)

At points in Ryder's childhood this car becomes the focal point of his denial; at others it becomes a place of refuge, its rear seat doubling as a "sanctuary" against the "troubles" raging on "inside the house" (264). In another example, Ryder recalls how, as a boy, he would give himself "training sessions" to learn how to enjoy being lonely, when he otherwise "felt a sense of panic and a need for the company of my parents." In time, these "training sessions" had "become a regular and important feature of my life" and had "acquired a certain ritual, so that as soon as I felt the earliest signs of my need to return home I would make myself go to a special spot along the lane . . . where I would remain standing for several minutes, fighting off my emotions." At such times Ryder's stoical regulation of his emotions even leads him to experience a "strange thrill" that accompanies his "growing fear and panic" (172).

Ryder constructs a fantasy of parental concern and domestic harmony—an "ideal of family happiness" (264), in which he is the focus of his parents' love and interest—in order to deny the bleak reality of his childhood. Ryder's tenacious fantasy that he is loved by his parents (and his fear that he is not) is most clearly revealed in his obsession with his "parents' imminent arrival in the city" (176) to witness his performance at Thursday evening's festivities. Tellingly, Ryder imagines their arrival in fairy-tale terms:

A picture entered my mind of my parents, of the two of them in the horse-drawn carriage approaching the clearing outside the concert hall. I could see the local people . . . breaking off their conversations and turning towards

the sound of horse hooves. . . . And then the gleaming
carriage would burst into the wash of lights. . . . And my
mother and my father would be peering out of the carriage
window, on their faces the first traces of excited anticipa-
tion. . . . (398)

Not despite but because of his parents' neglect the two become, in Merle Rubin's words, "the ultimate arbiters of his success."[23] Because Ryder is "about to perform once more before
my parents," he determines that his "priority," his "one central
objective," is "to ensure that my performance was the richest,
the most overwhelming of which I was capable" (420). Like
Stephan Hoffman, who is also set to perform before his parents
Thursday night, Ryder fears failing his mother and father above
all else. Remembering that his "parents were due shortly to arrive in the city," Ryder is seized with "an icy panic that was
almost tangible, the realisation that I had not prepared at all the
piece I was to perform before them this evening" (328).

It comes as little surprise to the reader, despite Ryder's repeated protestations of concern for his parents' well-being during their visit to the city to see him play ("And my poor parents,
coming all this way, to hear me perform for the very first time!"
[272]), that they do not show up at all—in fact, that they have
never come to see their world-class pianist son perform. Upon
realizing, after Thursday's event, "just how tenuous had been
the whole possibility of my parents' coming to town," Ryder
breaks down before Miss Stratmann, the organizer of his trip, at
whom he sobs, "Surely, it wasn't unreasonable of me to assume
they would come this time? After all, I'm at the height of my

powers now. How much longer am I supposed to go on travelling like this?" (512). Equally unsurprising is Ryder's next
move—Stevens-style—of allowing others to help him rebuild a
fantasy that has collapsed before his eyes. Sensing his despon-
dency over his parents' failure to show up, first Stratmann and
then a stranger Ryder encounters on a public tram recall (or more
probably fabricate) for Ryder a visit his parents made to the city
many years earlier, assuming that this story will ease the de-
spairing Ryder's emotional pain. Stratmann "remembers" his
parents as a "pleasant couple. Very kind and considerate to one
another," who were "happy the whole time they were here" (513).
She also recalls that they stayed in "an idyllic hotel" that no
longer exists, and then produces a photograph of this hotel, which
Ryder describes as looking "like a smaller version of the sort of
fairy-tale castle built by mad kings in the last century" (514–
15).

Ryder's fantasy that his family life was healthy and happy
(as a compensation for its desperation and his misery) is further
echoed in Boris's fantasy (as narrated by Ryder) of his family's
unity and harmony. In the "fantasy" that Ryder imagines Boris
has "been playing through over and over during the past weeks"
(218), the family is besieged by an army of "thugs" who assail
the house in well-organized waves of terror. Gustav and Boris
successfully fight off the thugs; and Boris later addresses the
defeated band of toughs, whom he conjectures come "from broken homes":

There's no sense in this fighting. You must all have had
homes once. Mothers and fathers. Perhaps brothers and

sisters. I want you to understand what's happening. These attacks of yours, your continual terrorising of our apartment, has meant that my mother is crying all of the time. She's always tense and irritable, and this means she often tells me off for no reason. It also means Papa has to go away for long periods, sometimes abroad, which Mother doesn't like. (220–21)

Gustav then exhorts the thugs to leave his family alone: "This was a very happy home before you started to terrorise it" (221–22). The story concludes with Ryder thanking Boris for rescuing the family: "Now things can be as they were. The way they were before" (222). In this escapist fantasy, tellingly, the family's problems come from without, not from within, and the son rescues the family from the grip of its problems. (This echoes in Stephan Hoffman's fantasy that he can rescue his family from its unhappiness.)

As one might expect, the dysfunctional qualities of Ryder's childhood family triangle are replicated in his adult family triangle. As Brooke Allen argues, Ryder "repeats the cycle of familial sickness that has blighted his own life" by taking "out his rage toward his parents on Sophie and little Boris."[24]

The chief sign of Ryder's emotional scarring and the principal cause of his blindness toward his family is his pronounced narcissism and egomania ("A town of this sort would be grateful for virtually anything I cared to offer it" [302]; "I could feel, almost physically, the tide of respect sweeping towards me" [201]). That Ryder is able to overlook the fact that the admiration shown him by others is largely feigned is revealed most clearly when he grants a local newspaper an interview and photo opportunity. Although it is clear that the journalists flatter his "unique charisma" (168) merely in order to gain the session, and that Ryder himself even knows this, he nevertheless takes their compliments seriously. Ryder overhears them refer to him as a "difficult shit," a "touchy bastard," and a "fool" (166, 167, 180), yet this does not stop him from agreeing to all of their requests, prompting Ryder to abandon Boris in a cafe for what appears to be hours. One journalist even advises the other, within earshot of Ryder, "remember, like all of these types, he's very vain. So pretend to be a big fan of his. . . . With these types, you just have to keep up the flattery. . . . Don't stop feeding his ego" (166–67).

Ryder's workaholism—he will disappoint Sophie and Boris but never his public—stems from this constant need to feed his own ego. Invariably, the public's demands come before his family's needs. For example, Ryder frequently abandons Sophie in order to do the bidding of Hoffman, Brodsky, or someone else associated with his official visit. And he tells Boris at one point:

I know you must be wondering. . . . why it is we can't just settle down and live quietly, the three of us. You must . . . wonder why I have to go away all the time, even though your mother gets upset about it. Well, you have to understand, the reason I keep going on these trips, it's not because I don't love you and dearly want to be with you. . . . I have to keep going on these trips because, you see, you can never tell when it's going to come along. I mean the very special one, the very important trip, the one that's very very important, not just for me but for everyone, everyone in the whole world. . . . You see, it would be so easy just to miss it. . . . And you see, once you miss it, there's no going back, it would be too late. . . . That's why I've got to carry on for the moment, keep travelling all the time. (217–18)

Vague, absurd, and hubristic, Ryder's comments to Boris reveal the narcissistic root of his workaholism and emotional instability. As in *The Remains of the Day,* Ishiguro is concerned here with "the ways in which role-playing, the fabrication of a public facade, can eviscerate the private self."[25]

Ryder's neglect of Sophie and Boris in the present mirrors his treatment by his mother and father in the past: Ryder offers false assurances to Boris and Sophie that things between them will be different—and better—in the near future (157, 446); he reveals his lack of fatherly concern for Boris (470–72), abandoning him temporarily at numerous points; and he blames Sophie for his emotional volatility—"I could sense things were in danger of slipping out of control again, and I felt returning some of the intense annoyance I had experienced earlier in the day about the way Sophie had brought such chaos into my life" (243). At other points he chastises Sophie "for the confusion she had brought into my affairs" (179) and for "reducing my carefully planned time-table to chaos" (289).

The single most revealing hint that Ryder's relationship with Boris and Sophie is dysfunctional is when Ryder and Boris go back to look for Boris's toy in their old apartment complex. There, they encounter a former neighbor who describes a family (probably Ryder, Sophie, and Boris) that recently vacated the apartment next door: "I felt sorry for them at times. . . . But when it goes on like that, well, you just want to see them go. . . . To be fair, I don't think there was physical violence. But still, when you had to listen to them shouting late at night, it was very upsetting. . . . He went away a lot, but from what we understood he had to, that was all part of his work . . ." (214–16). At the very least, this description hints at the kind of turmoil recently experienced among the three.

For all of his "concern" for their well-being, Ryder is incapable of bonding with Sophie and Boris during his visit to the city, which leaves him feeling alienated and lonely. Indeed, *The Unconsoled* ends with Sophie telling Ryder to "Go away"— "Leave us. You were always outside of our love"—and with her remarking to Boris that Ryder will "never be one of us": let him "go around the world, giving out his expertise and wisdom. He needs to do it. Let's just leave him to it now" (532). And at one point Miss Collins tells Ryder, "it really would be a great sadness to me if you were to continue making your mistakes over and over" (147), suggesting that this is not the first time Ryder has failed to bond with Sophie and Boris during a visit to the city. For this reason, perhaps, Pico Iyer concludes that the "real theme of this profoundly lonely and harrowing book is disconnection," that "everyone is ultimately locked inside his own concerns, deaf to everyone else, and doomed to shout his sorrows to the wind."[26] Iyer's reading is apt but can be extended: in Ishiguro's novel individuals do not have the level of control over their lives that they believe themselves or would like themselves to possess. At virtually every point in the text Ryder and the other characters fear a slip into chaos, whether perceptual or emotional.

The dysfunctional Ryder-Sophie-Boris triangle also mirrors the Leo Brodsky-Collins-Bruno relationship. Although they remain married, it has been two decades since Brodsky and Miss Collins have lived together. In the intervening years, Brodsky has thought of little but winning her back, even though his unappeased anger and drunkenness have led him to shout obscenities at her and even physically to attack her in public (318), driving her further away. "Brodsky-Collins-Bruno triangle" is stated intentionally, for the dog Bruno functions as a child-substitute for the ailing Brodsky. Mourning the recently deceased Bruno as if he were a child, Brodsky implores Collins in the hope of regaining her, "We never had children. So let's get an animal" (327): "We could keep an animal. We could love and care for it together. Perhaps that was what we didn't have before. . . . We never had children. So let's do this instead" (274). Brodsky hopes that Collins will once again become a "wonderful consolation" (313) in his otherwise unconsoled existence.

However, Brodsky is even more taken with his "wound"—an incarnation of his masochism and narcissism—than he is with his woman, music, or dog. Brodsky calls his wound "an old friend" (464), and uses it as an excuse for his drinking and impotence. "I was injured, very badly, many years ago," he observes, and the resulting wound "never healed properly" (308). Clearly, Brodsky's wound has become an end in itself, the principal focus of his life:

When I conducted my orchestra, I always touched my wound, caressed it. Some days I picked at its edges, even pressed it hard between the fingers. You realise soon enough when a wound's not going to heal. The music, even when I was a conductor, I knew that's all it was, just a consolation. It helped for a while. I liked the feeling, pressing the wound, it fascinated me. (313)

Brodsky's aesthetic fascination with his own pain is underscored when he advises a recent widow at her husband's funeral, "This is a precious time. Come. Caress your wound now. It will be there for the rest of your life. But caress it now, while it's raw and bleeding" (372). This fascination is also underscored when, after Brodsky's concert appearance Thursday evening, Collins accuses him of being nothing more than a "charlatan. A cowardly, irresponsible fraud," whose "music will only ever be about that silly little wound" (499): "That's your real love, Leo, that wound, the one true love of your life! . . . Me, the music, we're neither of us anything more to you than mistresses you seek consolation from. You'll always go back to your one real love. To that wound!" (498). At bottom, *The Unconsoled* suggests that narcissism and masochism—a self-absorbed, self-enclosed, self-hating addiction to pain and vanity—rule the contemporary artist's passions. As Ishiguro himself puts it, the unconsoled is "the artist, who, suffering some hurt in childhood, turns to art to find some consolation it can never provide."[27]

The above two triangles are echoed in the Hoffman-Christine-Stephan triangle. Like Ryder, the hotel manager Hoffman is an obsessive workaholic and "perfectionist" (25) whose hotel

THE UNCONSOLED

is his "life's work" (122). However, Hoffman's work, at least for the last two years, has also been to rehabilitate Brodsky, and, for the last two decades, to rehabilitate a relationship with his wife that he believes has been deteriorating. Also like the Ryder-Sophie relationship, the Hoffman-Christine one is fraught with masochism and miscommunication, and is dysfunctional in the extreme. Like Ryder, Christine fantasizes an ideal family, one "comfortable" (416) and "warm and close" (417), to counter the reality of her strained and cold and aloof one. And like Brodsky with Collins, Hoffman is obsessed with Christine, with whom, twenty-two years ago, a "very large misunderstanding" developed, for which Hoffman has been atoning since. The misunderstanding developed when Hoffman, without meaning to mislead her, gave the artistically sensitive Christine the impression that he was a composer of music. After lying to save face, claiming that he was merely taking a temporary break from composing in order to clear his mind, she discovered the truth, after which a "tension came into our lives." At first allowing himself to believe that he "was slowly winning her" back again by other means, Hoffman at last realizes that Christine would "leave me. Sooner or later. It was just a matter of time" (345–52). Thus, the Brodsky-Collins relationship is echoed in the Hoffman-Christine one, in which the fallen professional male is abandoned by an unappreciative wife, whose affection he seeks to regain by regaining his standing in the public eye.

Like Brodsky, Hoffman believes that his wife is innately superior to him, yet he nevertheless wishes to lose rather than to regain her. Believing himself to be a "mediocrity" to which his wife has been "chained" for years (354), Hoffman masochisti-

cally wishes to fail with her, just as he does with his job and his
Brodsky rehabilitation project. At a number of points in the novel
he even rehearses what he will say to Christine when he fails
her: I'm nothing but "an ox, an ox, an ox" (123, 383, 507).

That the self-destructive Hoffman wants it all "to fail" (441)
is suggested at many points. He attempts to throw Ryder off by
moving him from one hotel room to another, whenever he is
beginning to feel at home, and by arranging to have a distracting
"electronic scoreboard" (382) operating while Ryder fields questions from the public at Thursday evening's event. That Hoffman
wishes to unnerve his son is suggested by his repeated and sav-
age undermining of Stephan's confidence in his own piano playing. That he wishes to throw off Brodsky for his all-important
Thursday night performance is suggested by his denying Brodsky
the chance to meet with Collins (431) and by his offering the
alcoholic conductor a drink—"Just a little. It'll steady you"
(442)—immediately prior to the event. Although Hoffman is
aware that a "relapse" in Brodsky's "recovery" would be "a personal disaster" for me—It "would mark the end" and "be my
finish. A humiliating finish!" (427)—he nevertheless goes out
of his way to insure such a relapse. He then appears only too
happy to take all of the blame, telling Christine:

> The evening. It's a shambles. Why pretend it's anything
> else? Why continue to tolerate me? Year after year, blun-
> der after blunder. . . . Everyone, the whole city, knows
> who is responsible for tonight's proceedings. . . . Why was
> I ever allowed to put my clumsy hands anywhere near such
> divine things as music, art, culture? You, from a talented

family, you could have married anyone. What a mistake you made. A tragedy. But it's not too late for you. You are still beautiful. Why wait any longer? What further proof do you need? Leave me. Leave me. Find someone worthy of you. (506–7)

Like Brodsky, the would-be artist Hoffman succeeds only in driving away the one woman he claims to love, and is left nursing his wound. By failing once and for all with everyone, Hoffman can at last rid himself of—or affirm—the agony of his inadequacy.

Hoffman and Christine abuse not only each other, however, but their son, Stephan. Like Ryder, Stephan Hoffman must endure parents who make him feel responsible for their problems yet, paradoxically, unimportant. As Brooke Allen describes Stephan, "A gifted young pianist who is crushed by his egotistical parents might just be a version of Ryder as a youth."[28] Hoping to "make my parents proud tomorrow night" (160), Stephan finds himself rejected by parents who refuse to encourage him or even to remain in the audience for his successful performance. Instead, they intentionally make him feel like a mediocrity, a major disappointment, and a "laughing stock" (480) when it comes to his artistic abilities. Hoffman goes so far as to view his son as "an embodiment of the great mistake" Christine "made in her life" by marrying him (354), and thus insists on walking out of Stephan's performance Thursday evening because he cannot bear to see his only son "making a laughing stock of himself before the most distinguished citizens of this town" (506). Clearly, Hoffman is more concerned with his own staged rejection than with his son's well-being.

Like Ryder, Stephan counters this parental neglect and abuse by constructing a fantasy "that he would somehow perform at a level never before attained, and that he would finish to find his parents smiling, applauding and exchanging with each other looks of deep affection" (69):

> I had this fantasy of spending months somewhere locked away, practising and practising. My parents wouldn't see me for months and months. Then one day I'd suddenly come home. . . . go to the piano, lift the lid, start playing. . . . And they'd be standing there in the middle of the room . . . both of them completely astounded. . . . it's a fantasy I've had ever since I was thirteen or fourteen. (76)

"Parental abuse" is not stated here lightly: Stephan is made to believe that his parents' entire happiness and emotional well-being depends on how well he plays the piano, both when a child and as an adult. This expectation places a crushing burden on him, which he can only begin to lift by leaving town, as he eventually determines to do.

Interestingly, *The Unconsoled* concludes similarly to *Remains of the Day* in one significant sense: the protagonist turns his public and private failures into successes and persuades himself to continue down the same path he has been on. Despite Ryder's unsuccessful rapprochement with Sophie and Boris and his failure even to perform at Thursday's concert, he prepares to leave for his next engagement in Helsinki convinced that "Things had not, after all, gone so badly." Even though he ends up contributing nothing to the event and the townspeople no longer even seem to recognize him, Ryder nevertheless muses that "Whatever disappointments this city had brought, there was no doubting that my presence had been greatly appreciated" (534). Notably, he thinks these thoughts while circling the city in a tram, just as Stevens thinks similar thoughts while circling England in a car.

The Unconsoled was received less warmly than the author's earlier three novels. Amit Chaudhuri, for example, pronounced the work a "failure," even if failure "implies the presence of artistic vision and talent."[29] Other readers accused *The Unconsoled* of being a "talented mess"[30] or of being boring—a "static," undramatic work "heading nowhere except back into itself."[31] "One is not sure what exactly has been attempted" in this work, wrote Richard Rorty, "nor what has been achieved."[32] A probable reason for this cooler critical reception is that the book follows in the tradition of the "baggy monster" school of novel-writing while the earlier three books are far shorter, far less "messy" novels. Another reason is that it is Kafkaesque rather than Jamesian, rough-hewn rather than neatly chiseled. Some have confused this new departure with a shallow and dry or self-indulgent experimentalism. Ishiguro himself explains this departure in an interview that emerged shortly after the appearance of *Remains,* in which he declares an unsatisfied instinct for "brilliant messiness"; a desire to engage "the messy, chaotic, undisciplined side" of his writing; a desire to follow in the spirit of Dostoevsky rather than Chekhov: "I have these two god-like figures in my reading experience: Chekhov and Dostoevsky. So far, in my writing career, I've aspired more to the Chekhov: the spare and the precise, the carefully, controlled tone. But I do sometimes envy the utter mess, the chaos of Dostoevsky. He does reach some things that you can't reach in any other way. . . ."[33] Wishing to move away from the tonal realism and structural "perfection" of *Remains,* Ishiguro sought to render *The Unconsoled* "a messy, jagged, loud kind of book."[34]

On the other hand, other reviewers of *The Unconsoled* praised its author for his artistic daring—for revolutionizing his tone and structure—while remaining true to his earlier vision. As Vince Passaro observes, "Ishiguro retains here his loving eye for the arbitrary and deeply inhibiting social manners that have been the chief failing of the characters in all his books—a sense of formality that becomes a kind of willful blindness, a tendency toward doing absolutely the wrong thing for perfectly proper reasons."[35] And Rachel Cusk deemed *The Unconsoled* a "masterpiece" for the "originality of its conception, the scope of its intentions, and the precision with which they are executed."[36]

Kazuo Ishiguro has published four powerful, evocative, original novels to date and is already among the most closely followed British novelists of his generation. For all of their differences, Ishiguro's four novels share enough similarities—unreliable first-person narrators, protagonists who remake themselves by "mixing memory and desire," and emotional and psychological emphases—to suggest a coherence and integrity to the author's aesthetic vision. Moreover, in all of his novels Ishiguro eschews the temptation to create protagonists who resemble the author himself. As Ishiguro explains,

I've always found it easier to be intimate and revealing with central characters who are not like me. . . .
Partly it's to do with not being an exhibitionist . . . but
also I think it serves me as a form of artistic discipline.
When you're dealing with someone not like yourself,
you have to think much harder about why that person
behaves in certain ways, why certain things have happened to him or her. I think one of the dangers of having a kind of alter ego in fiction is that you drag in all
kinds of things that are irrelevant in an artistic sense
simply because they are things that you are concerned
with as a person yourself.[37]

Although Ishiguro distances himself from his characters,
the author's published comments about literary artists reveal
much about his protagonists, each of whom is an artist figure of
sorts, whether literally, as a painter or pianist, or figuratively, as
a narrator who gives subjective shape to reality and who recre-
ates him- or herself through narrative. As Ishiguro remarks of
writers,

I think a lot of them do write out of something that is unresolved somewhere deep down and, in fact, it's probably
too late ever to resolve it. Writing is a kind of consolation
or therapy. . . . It's a kind of consolation that the world
isn't quite the way you wanted it, but you can somehow
reorder it or try and come to terms with it by . . . creating
your own world and own version of it.[38]

Indeed, all of Ishiguro's protagonists are haunted by something "unresolved somewhere deep down"; all of them use their self-narratives as a "kind of consolation or therapy." For each of Ishiguro's narrators the world and the self are not quite as they should be; and each of them responds to this disappointment by fabricating narratives that pretend circumstances are otherwise. Perhaps this, above all, is Kazuo Ishiguro's master theme.

NOTES

Chapter One:
Understanding Kazuo Ishiguro

1. This prize, established in 1969, currently carries with it an award of twenty thousand pounds sterling.

2. Gregory Mason, "An Interview with Kazuo Ishiguro," *Contemporary Literature* 30 (1989): 336. Some of the material used in this chapter was derived from an extended telephone conversation with Ishiguro, 2 Aug. 1996.

3. Bill Bryson, "Between Two Worlds," *New York Times,* 29 Apr. 1990, sec. 6, p. 39.

4. Philip Hensher, "Books," *Harper's and Queen* (May 1995): 21.

5. Graham Swift, "Kazuo Ishiguro," *Bomb* (Fall 1989): 22.

6. Kenzaburo Oe and Kazuo Ishiguro, "The Novelist in Today's World: A Conversation," *Boundary 2* 18 (1991): 115.

7. Allan Vorda and Kim Herzinger, "An Interview with Kazuo Ishiguro," *Mississippi Review* 20 (1991): 134–35.

8. Vorda and Herzinger, 135.

9. Vorda and Herzinger, 139.

10. Swift, 22.

11. Stanley Kauffmann, "The Floating World," *The New Republic,* 6 Nov. 1995, 43.

12. Galen Strawson, "Tragically Disciplined and Dignified," *Times Literary Supplement,* 19–25 May 1989, 535.

13. Mason, 336.

14. Richard Rorty, "Consolation Prize," *Village Voice Literary Supplement,* Oct. 1995, 13.

15. Malcolm Bradbury, *The Modern British Novel* (London: Penguin Books, 1994), 424.

16. Vorda and Herzinger, 152.

17. Mason, 341.

18. Wayne Booth, *The Rhetoric of Fiction,* 2d ed. (Chicago: University of Chicago Press, 1983), 158–59.

19. Mason, 337.

20. Vorda and Herzinger, 135.

21. David Goldknopf, *The Life of the Novel* (Chicago: University of Chicago Press, 1972), 41.

22. Cynthia F. Wong, "The Shame of Memory: Blanchot's Self-Dispossession in Ishiguro's *A Pale View of Hills,*" *CLIO* 24 (1995): 144.

23. Bryson, 39.

24. Amit Chaudhuri, "Unlike Kafka," *London Review of Books,* 8 June 1995, 30.

25. Meera Tamaya, "Ishiguro's *Remains of the Day:* The Empire Strikes Back," *Modern Language Studies* 22 (1992): 45.

26. Oe and Ishiguro, 115.

27. Vorda and Herzinger, 142.

28. T. S. Eliot, *The Complete Poems and Plays, 1909–1950* (New York: Harcourt, Brace, and World, 1952), 37.

29. Mason, 342.

30. Mason, 338.

31. Mason, 347.

32. Mason, 347.

33. Sigmund Freud, *Five Lectures on Psycho-analysis* (New York: Norton, 1961), 22.

34. Swift, 23.

35. Bryson, 38.

36. Mason, 343.

37. Vorda and Herzinger, 147–48.

38. Oe and Ishiguro, 115.

39. Salman Rushdie, "What the Butler Didn't See," *The Observer,* 21 May 1989, 53.

40. Mason, 340.

41. Mason, 346. This comment of 1989 does not apply to the more openly experimental *The Unconsoled.*

42. Vorda and Herzinger, 145.

43. Vorda and Herzinger, 140, 149, 142.

44. Peter Wain, "The Historical-Political Aspect of the Novels of Kazuo Ishiguro," *Language and Culture* (Japan) 23 (1992): 193.

45. Joseph Frank, *The Widening Gyre: Crisis and Mastery in Modern Literature* (Bloomington: Indiana University Press, 1968), 19.

Chapter Two:
A Pale View of Hills

1. Penelope Lively, "Backwards and Forwards: Recent Fiction," *Encounter* (June–July 1982): 90.

2. Paul Bailey, "Private Desolations," *Times Literary Supplement,* 19 Feb. 1982, 179.

3. Peter Wain, "The Historical-Political Aspect of the Nov-

els of Kazuo Ishiguro," *Language and Culture* 23 (1992): 186.

4. Kazuo Ishiguro, *A Pale View of Hills* (New York: Vintage, 1990), 54. Further references are noted parenthetically in the text.

5. Cynthia F. Wong, "The Shame of Memory: Blanchot's Self-Dispossession in Ishiguro's *A Pale View of Hills," CLIO* 24 (1995): 143.

6. Fumio Yoshioka, "Beyond the Division of East and West: Kazuo Ishiguro's *A Pale View of Hills," Studies in English Literature* (1988): 77.

7. Yoshioka, 74.

8. Gregory Mason, "An Interview with Kazuo Ishiguro," *Contemporary Literature* 30 (1989): 338, 347.

9. Wain, 180.

10. James Joyce, *Dubliners* (New York: Viking Critical Library, 1976), 39.

11. Joyce, 40.

12. Joyce, 38.

13. Joyce, 39.

14. Joyce, 40.

15. Joyce, 41.

16. Wain, 180.

17. Mason, 337.

18. Yoshioka, 75.

19. Mason, 337.

20. Mason, 337.

21. Calvin S. Hall, *A Primer of Freudian Psychology* (New York: New American Library, 1954), 89.

22. Hall, 90.

23. Hall, 91.

24. Gabriele Annan, "On the High Wire," *New York Review of Books,* 7 Dec. 1989, 3.

25. Annan, 3.

26. Mason, 338.

27. Adrian Room, ed., *Room's Classical Dictionary* (London: Routledge and Keegan Paul, 1983), 282.

28. Joel Schmidt, ed., *Larousse Greek and Roman Mythology* (New York: McGraw-Hill, 1980), 255.

29. Yoshioka, 77.

30. Sigmund Freud, *New Introductory Lectures on Psychoanalysis* (New York: Norton, 1965), 105.

31. Sigmund Freud, *The Economic Problem of Masochism,* vol. 19 of *Standard Edition of the Complete Psychological Works of Sigmund Freud* (London: Hogarth Press and the Institute of Psychoanalysis, 1961), 169.

32. Freud, *Economic Problem of Masochism,* 169–70.

33. Sigmund Freud, *A Case of Homosexuality in a Woman,* vol. 18 of *Standard Edition of the Complete Psychological Works of Sigmund Freud* (London: Hogarth Press and the Institute of Psychoanalysis, 1955), 162–63.

34. Salman Rushdie, "What the Butler Didn't See," *The Observer,* 21 May 1989, 53.

35. Wong, 141.

36. Edith Milton, "In a Japan Like Limbo," *New York Times Book Review,* 9 May 1982, 13.

37. Yoshioka, 72.

Chapter Three:
An Artist of the Floating World

1. Nigel Hunt, "Two Close Looks at Faraway," *Brick: A Journal of Reviews,* no. 31 (Fall 1987): 37.

2. Peter Wain, "The Historical-Political Aspect of the Novels of Kazuo Ishiguro," *Language and Culture* 23 (1992): 193.

3. Kathryn Morton, "After the War was Lost," *New York Times Book Review,* 8 June 1986, 19.

4. Cynthia F. Wong, "The Shame of Memory: Blanchot's Self-Dispossession in Ishiguro's *A Pale View of Hills,*" *CLIO* 24 (1995): 143.

5. Patrick Parrinder, "Manly Scowls," *London Review of Books* (6 Feb. 1986): 16.

6. Kazuo Ishiguro, *An Artist of the Floating World* (New York: Vintage, 1989), 67. Further references are noted parenthetically in the text.

7. Parrinder, 16.

8. Parrinder, 16.

9. Graham Swift, "Kazuo Ishiguro," *Bomb* (Fall 1989): 23.

10. Hunt, 38.

11. Gregory Mason, "An Interview with Kazuo Ishiguro," *Contemporary Literature* 30 (1989): 340–42.

12. Wain, 187.

13. Wain, 187.

14. Morton, 19.

15. Allan Vorda and Kim Herzinger, "An Interview with Kazuo Ishiguro," *Mississippi Review* 20 (1991): 152.

16. Wain, 191.

17. Mason, 341.

18. Mason, 339, 341.

Chapter Four:
The Remains of the Day

1. Allan Vorda and Kim Herzinger, "An Interview with Kazuo Ishiguro," *Mississippi Review* 20 (1991): 142.

2. Gregory Mason, "An Interview with Kazuo Ishiguro," *Contemporary Literature* 30 (1989): 347.

3. Graham Swift, "Kazuo Ishiguro," *Bomb* (Fall 1989): 23.

4. John Kucich, *Repression in Victorian Literature: Charlotte Bronte, George Eliot, and Charles Dickens* (Berkeley: University of California Press, 1987), 2.

5. Sigmund Freud, *Five Lectures on Psycho-analysis* (New York: Norton, 1961), 43.

6. Kazuo Ishiguro, *The Remains of the Day* (New York: Vintage, 1993), 20. Further references are noted parenthetically in the text.

7. Kathleen Wall, "*The Remains of the Day* and Its Challenges to Theories of Unreliable Narration," *Journal of Narrative Technique* 24 (1994): 28–29.

8. Marshall Berman, *All That is Solid Melts into Air* (New York: Simon and Schuster, 1982), 106. I am indebted to Caroline Patey, "When Ishiguro Visits the West Country," *Acme* 44 (1991): 151, for making the Ishiguro-Berman connection.

9. Quoted in Berman, 108–9.

10. Frank E. Huggett, *Life Below Stairs: Domestic Servants in England from Victorian Times* (New York: Charles Scribner's Sons, 1977), 35, 46.

11. Salman Rushdie, "What the Butler Didn't See," *The Observer*, 21 May 1989, 53.

12. Ihab Hassan, "An Extravagant Reticence," *The World and I* 5, no. 2 (Feb. 1990): 374.

13. Kucich, 1.

14. Freud, *Five Lectures,* 21–22.

15. Freud, *Five Lectures,* 22.

16. Sigmund Freud, *Repression,* vol. 14 of *Standard Edition of the Complete Psychological Works of Sigmund Freud* (London: Hogarth Press and the Institute of Psychoanalysis, 1957), 147.

17. Compare this with Freud's claim that the "motive and purpose of repression" is "nothing else than the avoidance of unpleasure," in *Repression,* 153.

18. Patey, 150.

19. David Gurewich, "Upstairs, Downstairs," *The New Criterion* (Dec. 1989): 78.

20. Vorda and Herzinger, 153.

21. Cynthia F. Wong, "The Shame of Memory: Blanchot's Self-Dispossession in Ishiguro's *A Pale View of Hills,*" *CLIO* 24 (1995): 130.

22. Wall, 26.

23. Hassan, 370.

24. Mark Kamine, "A Servant of Self-Deceit," *The New Leader,* 13 Nov. 1989, 22.

25. Wall, 23–24.

26. Swift, 22.

27. Gurewich, 78.

28. Joseph Conrad, *The Collected Letters of Joseph Conrad,* vol. 2, Frederick R. Karl and Laurence Davies, eds. (Cambridge: Cambridge University Press, 1986), 108.

29. Vorda and Herzinger, 135–36.

30. Swift, 23.
31. Patey, 147.
32. Wall, 24.
33. As an example of the first instance: "One should not be looking back to the past so much. . . . It is essential . . . to keep one's attention focused on the present; to guard against any complacency creeping in on account of what one may have achieved in the past" (139). As an example of the second instance: "But I see I have become somewhat lost in these old memories. This had never been my intention, but then it is probably no bad thing if in doing so I have at least avoided becoming unduly preoccupied with the events of this evening . . ." (159).
34. Hassan, 373.
35. Gurewich, 80.
36. Vorda and Herzinger, 142.
37. Hassan, 374.
38. Meera Tamaya, "Ishiguro's *Remains of the Day:* The Empire Strikes Back," *Modern Language Studies* 22 (1992): 54.
39. He notes a "sharp decline in professional standards" of late (7); observes that the staff at Darlington Hall has dwindled from twenty-eight to four persons over the years; and points out that when he takes his excursion "Darlington Hall would probably stand empty for the first time this century" (23).
40. Stevens notes that Darlington Hall has been purchased by Americans after "two centuries" in "the hands of the Darlington family" (6); observes that Americans are "the only ones that can afford" grand old English homes (242); and takes his excursion in Farraday's American Ford.

41. Gurewich, 78–79.
42. Hassan, 372–73.
43. Vorda and Herzinger, 139–40.

Chapter Five:
The Unconsoled

1. Kazuo Ishiguro, *The Unconsoled* (New York: Knopf, 1995), 383. Further references are noted parenthetically in the text.

2. Stanley Kauffmann, "The Floating World," *The New Republic,* 6 Nov. 1995, 45.

3. Richard Rorty, "Consolation Prize," *Village Voice Literary Supplement,* Oct. 1995, 13.

4. Amit Chaudhuri, "Unlike Kafka," *London Review of Books,* 8 June 1995, 30.

5. Paul Bailey, "Private Desolations," *Times Literary Supplement,* 19 Feb. 1982, 179.

6. Pico Iyer, "The Butler Didn't Do It, Again," *Times Literary Supplement,* 28 Apr. 1995, 22.

7. Merle Rubin, "Probing the Plight of Lives 'Trapped' in Others' Expectations," *Christian Science Moniter,* 4 Oct. 1995, 14.

8. Rubin, 14.

9. Iyer, 22.

10. Vince Passaro, "New Flash from an Old Island," *Harpers,* Oct. 1995, 73.

11. Quoted in Kauffmann, 44. In this connection, Pico Iyer deems the novel "a Kafkaesque horror story made to play like

social comedy" (22); Nick Sweet, "Kafka Set to Music," *Contemporary Review* (Oct. 1995), writes that "*The Unconsoled* simply reeks of Kafka" (223); and Stanley Kauffmann observes that Ishiguro's novel shares with Kafka's novels a distinctive "spectral humor" (45). What Milan Kundera, *The Art of the Novel* (New York: Harper and Row, 1988), says of Kafka's work is also true of Ishiguro's novel: "The *Kafkan* is not restricted to either the private or the public domain; it encompasses both. The public is the mirror of the private, the private reflects the public" (112).

12. Passaro, 73.

13. Sigmund Freud, *The Uncanny,* vol. 17 of *Standard Edition of the Complete Psychological Works of Sigmund Freud* (London: Hogarth Press and the Institute of Psychoanalysis, 1955), 221.

14. Freud, *The Uncanny,* 251.

15. Kauffmann, 44.

16. Freud, *The Uncanny,* 219.

17. Freud, *The Uncanny,* 220, my emphasis.

18. Freud, *The Uncanny,* 237.

19. Freud, *The Uncanny,* 248.

20. Passaro, 75.

21. Philip Hensher, "Books," *Harper's and Queen* (May 1995): 21.

22. Kathleen Wall, "*The Remains of the Day* and Its Challenges to Theories of Unreliable Narration," *Journal of Narrative Technique* 24 (1994): 29.

23. Rubin, 14.

24. Brooke Allen, "Leaving Behind Daydreams for Night-

mares," *Wall Street Journal,* 11 Oct. 1995, A12.

    25. Rubin, 14.

    26. Iyer, 22.

    27. Quoted in Hensher, 21.

    28. Allen, A12.

    29. Chaudhuri, 31.

    30. Roz Kaveney, "Tossed and Turned," *New Statesman and Society,* 12 May 1995, 39.

    31. Ned Rorem, "Fiction in Review," *Yale Review* 84 (1996): 159.

    32. Rorty, 13.

    33. Graham Swift, "Kazuo Ishiguro," *Bomb* (Fall 1989): 23.

    34. Allan Vorda and Kim Herzinger, "An Interview with Kazuo Ishiguro," *Mississippi Review* 20 (1991): 153.

    35. Passaro, 74.

    36. Rachel Cusk, "Journey to the End of the Day," *Times,* 11 May 1995, 38.

    37. Bill Bryson, "Between Two Worlds," *New York Times,* 29 April 1990, sec. 6, p. 39.

    38. Vorda and Herzinger, 151.

BIBLIOGRAPHY

Works by Kazuo Ishiguro

Novels

An Artist of the Floating World. London: Faber and Faber; New York: G. P. Putnam's Sons, 1986. Reprint. New York: Vintage, 1989.

A Pale View of Hills. London: Faber and Faber; New York: G. P. Putnam's Sons, 1982. Reprint. New York: Vintage, 1990.

The Remains of the Day. London: Faber and Faber; New York: Knopf, 1989. Reprint. New York: Vintage, 1993.

The Unconsoled. London: Faber and Faber; New York: Knopf, 1995. Reprint. New York: Vintage, 1996.

Stories and Film Script

"A Family Supper." *Esquire* (March 1990): 207–11.

"Getting Poisoned." In *Introduction 7: Stories by New Writers,* 38–51. London: Faber and Faber, 1981.

"A Strange and Sometimes Sadness." In *Introduction 7: Stories by New Writers,* 13–27. London: Faber and Faber, 1981.

"Summer After the War." *Granta* 7 (1983): 120–37.

"Waiting for J." In *Introduction 7: Stories by New Writers,* 28–37. London: Faber and Faber, 1981.

"The Goumet" (film script). *Granta* 43 (1993): 89–127.

BIBLIOGRAPHY

Works about Kazuo Ishiguro

Reviews

Allen, Brooke. "Leaving Behind Daydreams for Nightmares." *Wall Street Journal,* 11 October 1995, A12. Treats *The Unconsoled* within the context of Ishiguro's earlier, superficially less experimental novels.

Annan, Gabriele. "On the High Wire." *New York Review of Books,* 7 December 1989, 3–4. An overview of Ishiguro's first three novels.

Bailey, Paul. "Private Desolations." *Times Literary Supplement,* 19 February 1982, 179. Focuses on *A Pale View of Hills*'s narrative subtlety.

Chaudhuri, Amit. "Unlike Kafka." *London Review of Books,* 8 June 1995, 30–31. Compares *The Unconsoled* to Kafka's works and finds Ishiguro's novel wanting.

Cusk, Rachel. "Journey to the End of the Day." *Times,* 11 May 1995, 38. An appreciative review of *The Unconsoled,* focusing on its dreamlike quality.

Gurewich, David. "Upstairs, Downstairs." *The New Criterion* (December 1989): 77–80. Explores *The Remains of the Day* from the perspective of class and nationality.

Hassan, Ihab. "An Extravagant Reticence." *The World and I* 5, no. 2 (February 1990): 369–74. An insightful appreciation of *The Remains of the Day.*

Hunt, Nigel. "Two Close Looks at Faraway." *Brick: A Journal of Reviews,* no. 31 (Fall 1987): 36–38. Focuses on personal relationships in *An Artist of the Floating World.*

Iyer, Pico. "The Butler Didn't Do It, Again." *Times Literary*

Supplement, 28 April 1995, 22. Appreciative review of *The Unconsoled,* "one of the strangest novels in memory," by a fellow novelist.

Kamine, Mark. "A Servant of Self-Deceit." *The New Leader,* 13 November 1989, 21–22. Focuses on the Stevens-Kenton relationship in *The Remains of the Day.*

Kauffmann, Stanley. "The Floating World." *The New Republic,* 6 November 1995, 42–45. Appreciative review of *The Unconsoled,* within the context of Ishiguro's earlier novels, by a respected film critic.

Kaveney, Roz. "Tossed and Turned." *New Statesman and Society,* 12 May 1995, 39. Charges *The Unconsoled* with being a "talented mess of a novel."

Lively, Penelope. "Backwards and Forwards: Recent Fiction." *Encounter* (June–July 1982): 86–91. Emphasizes the emotional and psychological depth of *A Pale View of Hills.*

Milton, Edith. "In a Japan Like Limbo." *New York Times Book Review,* 9 May 1982, 12–13. Overplays the significance of historical background in *A Pale View of Hills.*

Morton, Kathryn. "After the War was Lost." *New York Times Book Review,* 8 June 1986, 19. Shows how *An Artist of the Floating World* teaches its audience "to read more perceptively."

Parrinder, Patrick. "Manly Scowls." *London Review of Books,* 6 February 1986, 16–17. An appreciative overview of *An Artist of the Floating World.*

Passaro, Vince. "New Flash from an Old Island." *Harpers,* October 1995, 71–75. Focuses on the literary influences of *The Unconsoled.*

Rorem, Ned. "Fiction in Review." *Yale Review* 84 (1996): 154–
59. A dismissive review of *The Unconsoled* that misses the
novel's irony.

Rorty, Richard. "Consolation Prize." *Village Voice Literary
Supplement,* October 1995, 13. A world-famous philoso-
pher expresses "appreciative puzzlement" over *The
Unconsoled.*

Rubin, Merle. "Probing the Plight of Lives 'Trapped' in Others'
Expectations." *Christian Science Moniter,* 4 October 1995,
14. Explores the social dimension of *The Unconsoled.*

Rushdie, Salman. "What the Butler Didn't See." *The Observer,*
21 May 1989, 53. A perceptive overview of *The Remains of
the Day.*

Strawson, Galen. "Tragically Disciplined and Dignified." *Times Literary Supplement,* 19–25 May 1989, 535. Treats *The Remains
of the Day* as a novel about the failure of communication.

Sweet, Nick. "Kafka Set to Music." *Contemporary Review* (October 1995): 223–24. Focuses too narrowly on *The
Unconsoled*'s debt to Kafka.

Articles

King, Bruce. "The New Internationalism: Shiva Naipaul, Salman
Rushdie, Buchi Emecheta, Timothy Mo, and Kazuo Ishiguro."
In *The British and Irish Novel Since 1960,* edited by James
Acheson, 192–211. New York: St Martin's Press, 1991. Un-
informative.

Mason, Gregory. "Inspiring Images: The Influence of the Japanese Cinema on the Writings of Kazuo Ishiguro." *East West
Film Journal* 3 (1989): 39–52. Explores a neglected influence.

BIBLIOGRAPHY

O'Brien, Susie. "Serving a New World Order: Postcolonial Politics in Kazuo Ishiguro's *The Remains of the Day*." *Modern Fiction Studies* 42 (1996): 787–806. A provocative postcolonial reading of the novel and the film.

Patey, Caroline. "When Ishiguro Visits the West Country: An Essay on *The Remains of the Day*." *Acme* (Italy) 44 (1991): 135–55. A perceptive if eccentric treatment of language and psychology in Ishiguro's best-known novel.

Rothfork, John. "Zen Comedy in Postcolonial Literature: Kazuo Ishiguro's *The Remains of the Day*." *Mosaic* 29 (1996): 79–102. Unconvincing.

Tamaya, Meera. "Ishiguro's *Remains of the Day:* The Empire Strikes Back." *Modern Language Studies* 22 (1992): 45–56. Examines Ishiguro's most famous novel from a postcolonial perspective.

Wain, Peter. "The Historical-Political Aspect of the Novels of Kazuo Ishiguro." *Language and Culture* (Japan) 23 (1992): 177–205. Useful summaries of the novels.

Wall, Kathleen. "*The Remains of the Day* And Its Challenges to Theories of Unreliable Narration." *Journal of Narrative Technique* 24 (1994): 18–42. Reads Ishiguro's most famous novel through the prism of narrative theory.

Wong, Cynthia F. "The Shame of Memory: Blanchot's Self-Dispossession in Ishiguro's *A Pale View of Hills*." *CLIO* 24 (1995): 127–45. Illuminating discussion of the use of memory and narratives of self in Ishiguro's first novel.

Yoshioka, Fumio. "Beyond the Division of East and West: Kazuo Ishiguro's *A Pale View of Hills*." *Studies in English Literature* (Japan) (1988): 71–86. Useful if unfocused close-reading of Ishiguro's first novel.

BIBLIOGRAPHY

Interviews and Profiles

Bradbury, Malcolm. *The Modern British Novel,* 423–25. London: Penguin Books, 1994. Ishiguro's creative writing teacher briefly surveys Ishiguro's novels within the context of contemporary Anglo-Asian literature.

Bryson, Bill. "Between Two Worlds." *New York Times,* 29 April 1990, sec. 6, pp. 38–39, 44, 80. An informative profile of and interview with Ishiguro centering on his choice of a career as novelist.

Hensher, Philip. "Books." *Harper's and Queen* (May 1995): 21. Excellent, brief discussion of Ishiguro's new artistic departures in *The Unconsoled.*

Krider, Dylan Otto. "Rooted in a Small Space: An Interview with Kazuo Ishiguro." *Kenyon Review* 20 (1998): 146–54. Centers on *The Unconsoled.*

Mason, Gregory. "An Interview with Kazuo Ishiguro." *Contemporary Literature* 30 (1989): 335–47. Focuses on the psychological dimensions of Ishiguro's novels.

Oe, Kenzaburo, and Kazuo Ishiguro. "The Novelist in Today's World: A Conversation." *Boundary 2: An International Journal of Literature and Culture* 18 (1991): 109–22. Reprinted as "Wave Patterns: A Dialogue" in *Grand Street* 10 (1991): 75–91. A less-than-illuminating discussion between the Nobel Prize–winning Japanese novelist Oe and Ishiguro.

Sinclair, Clive. "Kazuo Ishiguro." *The Roland Collection.* Video interview.

Stevenson, Randall. *A Reader's Guide to the Twentieth-Century Novel in Britain.* 130–36. Lexington, KY: University Press of Kentucky, 1993. Ishiguro's novels discussed within the context of non-native English writing.

BIBLIOGRAPHY

Swift, Graham. "Kazuo Ishiguro." *Bomb* (Fall 1989): 22–23, 29.
A dynamic, brief interview with a fellow novelist following
the publication of *The Remains of the Day.*
Vorda, Allan, and Kim Herzinger. "An Interview with Kazuo
Ishiguro." *Mississippi Review* 20 (1991): 131–54. Reprinted
as "Stuck on the Margins: An Interview with Kazuo Ishiguro"
in *Face to Face: Interviews with Contemporary Novelists,*
1–36. Houston: Rice University Press, 1993. The best interview yet published, wide-ranging and penetrating.

Index

The index does not include references to material in the notes.

INDEX

INDEX

INDEX